THE
ARMED FORCES

Practical guides for practical people

In this increasingly sophisticated world the need for manually skilled people to build our homes, cut our hair, fix our boilers, and make our cars go is greater than ever. As things progress, so the level of training and competence required of our skilled manual workers increases. In this new series of career guides from Trotman we look in detail at what it takes to train for, get into, and be successful at a wide spectrum of practical careers.

The *Real Life Guides* aim to inform and inspire young people and adults alike by providing comprehensive yet hard-hitting and often blunt information about what it takes to succeed in these careers.

Other titles in the series include:

THE BEAUTY INDUSTRY

CARPENTRY & CABINET-MAKING

CATERING

CONSTRUCTION

ELECTRICIAN

ENGINEERING TECHNICIAN

HAIRDRESSING

INFORMATION & COMMUNICATIONS TECHNOLOGY

THE MOTOR INDUSTRY

PLUMBING

THE POLICE SERVICE

RETAILING

SPORT & ACTIVE LEISURE

TRAVEL & TOURISM

WORKING OUTDOORS

WORKING WITH ANIMALS & WILDLIFE

WORKING WITH YOUNG PEOPLE

REAL life GUIDES

THE
ARMED FORCES

2nd Edition

NICK HIGGINS & ROSE MILLER

Real Life Guide to The Armed Forces

This second edition published in 2009 by Trotman Publishing, an imprint of Crimson Publishing Ltd, Westminster House, Kew Road, Richmond, Surrey TW9 2ND

First edition by Nick Higgins published in 2004 by Trotman & Company Ltd.

Authors: Nick Higgins and Rose Miller

© Trotman Publishing 2009

Design by Nicki Averill

British Library Cataloguing in Publication Data
A catalogue record for this book is available from the British Library

ISBN 978-1-84455-197-2

Typeset by RefineCatch Ltd, Bungay, Suffolk

Printed and bound in Italy by LEGO SpA

CONTENTS

ABOUT THE AUTHORS

A graduate in economics from Cambridge University, Nick Higgins is a writer specialising in careers and educational advice and recruitment communications campaigns. He has researched, written, edited or contributed to more than 40 publications and websites, including the *Guardian*, *From Learning to Earning*, *Careers-Portal*, the *A–Z of Exam Survival* and *Shine* magazine. He has also worked extensively with the British Army, writing the award-winning Territorial Army website and CD-ROM, and is currently heavily involved in the new Metropolitan Police Careers website.

Rose Miller is a qualified Careers Guidance specialist and teacher, with over 20 years of experience in assisting young people and adults to make career decisions. She has written education-industry activities for schools and delivered a wide range of training activities to careers guidance professionals working in a range of locations, including colleges, Connexions, the voluntary sector and prisons.

A graduate in English and Communication Studies from Liverpool University, she is currently studying an MA in Literature, Politics and Identity at the University of Worcester.

INTRODUCTION

It can't have escaped your attention that the Armed Forces are currently playing a very prominent role in world events. The size and scope of the British Army, Royal Navy and Royal Air Force (RAF) are expanding. As the Armed Forces grow, so do the number and range of career opportunities they provide.

But what exactly does that mean? Everyone has a preconceived idea of what it is to work for the Armed Forces. It's very easy to dismiss the services as a career option – perhaps you think it would be too difficult, or maybe you think you're overqualified or are nervous about going to war. On the other hand, it's just as easy to get overenthusiastic about the prospect of joining up without really appreciating what it would be like or whether it's really for you.

The Armed Forces certainly are not like they are often portrayed in movies or on television – even on the news! The stories and images you have seen may reflect one small part of the services, but they almost never let you in on the bigger picture. In reality, the services are diverse and complex organisations that draw on the latest technologies and training techniques to fulfil an array of important roles and responsibilities.

This book aims to paint that bigger picture – to open your eyes to the sheer variety of possibilities a career in the Armed Forces could have in store for you. It will help you to decide whether you are suited to the Army, Navy or Air Force and give you a few ideas of where exactly you might fit in. Finally, it will point you in the direction of further sources of useful information.

CHAPTER 1
SUCCESS STORY

FLIGHT LIEUTENANT JULES FLEMING

Pilot

On her 17th birthday, Flight Lieutenant Jules Fleming took to the skies and discovered a natural ability for flying. Spurred on by this experience, Jules applied for a flying scholarship, and the rest, as they say, is history. Now a true high-flyer in the RAF, Jules is a fast jet pilot on the Tornado GR4, based at RAF Marham in Norfolk. Outside of work she is an accomplished showjumper, badminton player and occasional motor-car racer.

Aged just 14, Jules Fleming decided that she wanted a job with a difference and was sure that a military career could offer just that. On her 17th birthday, Jules' father, an instructor at Retford Airfield, gave Jules a lesson in flying and from that moment it became evident in which direction her career should take her.

Encouraged to pursue this newly found talent, Jules applied for a flying scholarship. A year later, she had earned her private pilot's licence and become even further convinced about a career in flying. Based on this achievement, Jules applied to the RAF to become a pilot and recalls:

'I had always thought I would join the Army, but when my father suggested I should think about a career in flying it seemed the RAF offered the most opportunities.

I was 20 when I started initial officer training and this was followed by joint elementary training at RAF Church Fenton. From there I was streamed into fast jet and continued my training on the Tocano aircraft at RAF Linton-on-Ouse, North Yorkshire. This was followed by advanced fast jet training on the Hawk aircraft at RAF Valley in Wales. At the end of this we were assessed again and I was one of the few retained on the Squadron to become an instructor.'

Despite recognising the honour of being selected to continue as an instructor at RAF Valley, Jules was keen to get out on the front line and do the job she was trained for, she explains:

'It was a bizarre mix of emotions. I knew it was a huge compliment to be retained as an instructor before my career had really got going but equally I was eager to get out there and be on the front line. But like everything in life I believe in making the best of what you've got and I enjoyed the rest of my time at RAF Valley.'

After 2.5 years of instructing, Jules went back to training on the Tornado GR4 with 15 Squadron at RAF Lossiemouth. After an arduous eight months learning all the skills required to be an Operational Pilot she was posted to a front-line Squadron at RAF Marham. Describing her working day she says:

'There is no typical day for me but I can be expected to fly at anytime between 06.00 and 20.00 in all weather conditions ... We also do regular emergency handling training in the flight simulator.

From planning the flight, to the de-brief when we land, takes roughly eight hours. There is also time built in for physical exercise and team sport, such as indoor football, because it is essential that our fitness levels are maintained for flying.'

And Jules is no stranger to physical fitness outside of work either. An accomplished showjumper, Jules represents the RAF in this sport and recently competed in front of an audience which included Her Majesty the Queen at Royal Windsor.

Also demonstrating her keen sense of competition, Jules achieved an admirable fourth place at the televised Formula Women's motor racing competition held in 2004. Selected from an initial 10,000 applicants, Jules was considered talented enough on the race course to join the final 16 women to compete in this prestigious competition. She concedes:

'I guess I am an adrenalin junkie both inside and outside of work. I get just as much of a buzz when I am jumping over fences on my horse or racing round the track as I do when I'm on a low-level battle sortie, on a nighttime flying exercise.'

And in October 2008 Jules was challenged physically and mentally one step further when she completed a six-week detachment to the Gulf on Op Telic. Flying the Tornado GR4 on Close Air Support missions (CAS) and providing support to the military personnel on the ground, Jules relished flying on the front line and protecting the troops below her. She explains:

'I joined the RAF to fly on the front line and it's what I've been waiting to do since my fast jet training. Being in the Gulf was everything I expected – hot humid conditions, long exhausting night shifts – but a very rewarding experience. Knowing that we were helping to protect personnel on the ground and that we were there for them in the event of an emergency was a good feeling.'

Her advice to anyone considering a job in the RAF is simple:

'Just be yourself, make the best of what you have got, and have the confidence that you will succeed. I left school with mediocre A level grades but I didn't let that stop me and now I've achieved more than I could have ever anticipated. A military career also offers opportunities for sport that most other jobs just wouldn't. For instance, I don't think I would have been showjumping in front of the Queen at Windsor if I hadn't joined the RAF and it was a fantastic experience.'

3

RAF PILOT JOB DESCRIPTION

Your role as a pilot in the RAF is as varied as the aircraft you can fly. Once you've completed initial training, you'll be selected to fly jets, larger multi-engine aircraft or helicopters. As the pilot of a Eurofighter Typhoon, your primary role will be air-to-air combat or ground attack. In a Hercules transport aircraft, you could be sent anywhere in the world on military support or humanitarian aid missions. In a helicopter, your duties might include anything from search and rescue flights to ferrying troops and equipment into combat zones.

DID YOU KNOW?

There are over 50 career opportunities in the RAF. For further information call 0845 605 5555 or www.raf.mod.uk/careers.

After your initial training, you'll then receive further training on the aircraft type you've been assigned to, then start getting to grips with using that aircraft in your day-to-day job.

RAF PILOT ENTRY REQUIREMENTS

Qualifications: 5 GCSEs/SCEs and 2 A levels or 3 Highers or equivalent. GCSEs/SCEs at Grade C/3 minimum to include English Language and Maths.

Other requirements: Pilots must be the right measurement and build to fit an ejector seat, so judgement is made on a case-by-case basis. Sitting height, leg length and reach length are also measured. Eyesight, colour perception and hearing tests are carried out.

Joining age: 17.5–23

Pay after training: £33,050

Usual service: 18 years or up to the age of 38

Open to: men or women

CHAPTER 2
WHAT'S THE STORY?

If you're thinking of joining one of the three British Armed Forces, you should know what you could be getting yourself into. Being a serviceman or -woman isn't a job like any other – you're choosing a unique and demanding way of life that is shaped by the basic reasons for having a defence force. Your first consideration should be how much you buy into these reasons. Can you see yourself contributing to the mission?

THE MISSION

The Armed Forces exist to defend the United Kingdom (UK), its overseas territories, its people and its interests, and to act as a 'force for good' by strengthening international peace and security. That is the mission – one that is achieved through providing services and capabilities that not only meet the needs of today but also prepare for the future. This means having a body of highly trained and motivated servicemen and -women who are able to do whatever is needed of them – unquestioningly and at a moment's notice.

The key interest that the British Armed Forces work so hard to defend is ongoing peace and stability throughout mainland Europe. Without this, the security and prosperity of the UK itself would be at risk. However, in today's 'global village', our interests extend far beyond the borders of Europe, and the Armed

---

Q DID YOU KNOW?

The impact that the Armed Forces have had on our history is immense. Many phrases used today originate from the military, e.g. 'three square meals' comes from the early 19th century, when sailors were served their food on square plates.

Forces must be in a position to respond to any international incidents that may affect our lives – whatever they are, wherever they occur.

This could be a direct military threat to our shores – something which, thankfully, we haven't seen since the Second World War – or to our 14 overseas territories, as was the case when Argentina invaded the Falkland Islands in 1982. It could also be the existence of a dangerous regime or unstable region that serves to undermine international peace in general. For example, the Balkans conflict of the 1990s was in danger of spilling over onto a wider stage before NATO (North Atlantic Treaty Organisation) forces moved in, while in 2001 the Taliban regime in Afghanistan was known to be harbouring international terrorists. Other threats to international stability include ethnic and religious tension, environmental problems, competition for land and resources, organised crime (particularly drug trafficking) and so on. Such problems may not call for full military action, but by providing humanitarian and peacekeeping forces, the British Armed Forces are able to help prevent relatively minor situations from escalating into something far more dangerous. Already we can see that the Armed Forces are not just about going to war.

MAKING A DIFFERENCE

The popular image of the Armed Forces is one of charging into war, and for many hundreds of years that is generally all they were used for. Indeed, being 'ready for war' is still the main point of having an army, navy and air force, but readiness is more often than not a way of deterring hostile action than actually defending against it. From time to time forces are called into action. For example, the two Gulf conflicts of the last 15 years and the Falklands crisis in the early 1980s all represented major mobilisations of personnel and equipment from all three services.

However, there is a lot more to the modern Armed Forces than being ready for, or embarking on, a full-scale war. Through NATO and the United Nations (UN), Britain's Armed Forces are currently making positive contributions to the quality of people's lives all over the world, reducing the potential for instability in the process. For example, there are many British servicemen and women in Bosnia and Kosovo (in the Balkans), contributing to the NATO peacekeeping effort that is helping to provide the kind of safe environment necessary to rebuild a country after a destructive conflict; after severe flooding devastated Mozambique in 2000, the Royal Navy and RAF provided ships and helicopters to help give life-saving support to the country's people; and during the summer of 2001 about 2,000 British troops took part in an operation to collect more than 3,500 weapons from the ethnic Albanian population of Macedonia in a successful attempt to prevent further fighting between them and the rival Slavs.

DID YOU KNOW?

As part of their duties, the Royal Navy and Royal Air Force are called upon to provide search and rescue services around the coasts and mountains of the UK. Without them, thousands of people would be left stranded – potentially fatally – every year.

Such peacekeeping and humanitarian work is a major part of what the Armed Forces do and isn't restricted to foreign countries alone. There are plenty of opportunities for the services to make a difference in the UK as well. Just think back to the firefighters' strike of 2002, when the Army's Green Goddess fire engines hit the streets in an effort to cover for the regular service, and you'll start to build a picture of just how much the Armed Forces do, both at home and abroad.

WHERE IN THE WORLD?

The very nature of the Armed Forces' responsibilities takes them, and the people that serve in them, to all four corners of the world – and back again. The precise nature of these 'trips' abroad varies. Sometimes they are training exercises, sometimes minor short-term operations, sometimes large-scale mobilisations and sometimes permanent postings.

First and foremost, while the days of the British Empire covering three-quarters of the globe are long since over, the UK still has 14 overseas territories to defend just as keenly as mainland Britain. A number of these, including Gibraltar and the Falkland Islands, have their own permanent garrisons or detachments of troops, as do non-British territories Cyprus, Ascension Island in the southern Atlantic and Diego Garcia in the middle of the Indian Ocean. Other territories, such as the British Virgin Islands, aren't quite big enough for that kind of presence, but they (and their neighbours) do benefit from other kinds of support and protection. For instance, the Royal Navy has assisted with disaster relief in the aftermath of such events as the Indonesian tsunami of 2004 and the South Asia earthquake of 2005, and the hurricanes Gustav and Ike in the Cayman Islands, Turks and Caicos Islands. The Royal Frigate HMS *Northumberland* helped to deliver food aid to Somalia as part of Operation Atlanta (the European Union's first military expedition of naval forces).

DID YOU KNOW?

The last 5 years have seen British Armed Forces personnel deployed to more than 30 territories worldwide, including Brunei, Iraq, Canada, Turkey, Italy, Sierra Leone, Kosovo and East Timor.

The Armed Forces also have a permanent or semi-permanent presence in countries and areas that are either strategically important or provide the right kind of environment for training purposes. For example, the Army uses the lush rainforest of Belize in Central America for its jungle warfare training and, along with the RAF, has a garrison in Germany.

The Royal Navy contributes to Standing Naval Forces in the Mediterranean and North Atlantic, and has a dedicated fuelling and support party in Diego Garcia. But, of course, that's not to say that there's no one back home! You will find Army, Naval and RAF bases and personnel all over the UK, from Belfast to Wiltshire.

WORKING TOGETHER

Being a member of one of the Armed Forces is all about being part of a team, a collection of highly skilled and disciplined individuals working together to deliver a service that is far more than the sum of its parts. The same view can be taken of the three services themselves – that is, the Army, Navy and Air Force. When they work together as a team, it's called 'operating jointly', or 'jointery'. Jointery is by no means a new concept. The Roman general and future Roman emperor Julius Caesar invaded Britain using both land and sea forces, and probably would have included air power in his plans had it been invented! Fast-forward nearly 2,000 years, and D-Day, the turning point of the Second World War, would not have been the success it was were it not for the different branches of the Armed Forces working together so well.

However, such a joint approach is particularly relevant today, as advances in technology have made the traditional differences between the three services and their theatres of operations less and less relevant.

For instance, ships and submarines out at sea can now join the efforts of the Army

DID YOU KNOW?

The Royal Naval Air Station at Yeovilton in Somerset keeps several birds of prey to scare away smaller birds and keep the airfield clear.

infantry by launching cruise-missile attacks on targets hundreds of miles inland. Ships can also provide a platform from which to launch land forces ashore, as well as aircraft and helicopters, which in turn provide ground troops with air cover, transport and assistance in targeting enemy positions. All three services must join forces to combat the increased usage of the kinds of electronic, information and cyber warfare that pay no attention at all to whether the target is on land, sea or in the air.

Indeed, it's now unthinkable for a major operation not to involve more than one service. The 2003 coalition action against Iraq was a demonstration of what can be achieved when modern air, sea and ground capabilities are seamlessly combined.

WHAT NEXT?

The world and the challenges facing the Armed Forces never stop changing. This has always been true, which is why the work of the Army, Navy and RAF is as much about preparing for what may happen in the future as it is about reacting to situations today. To this end, the Ministry of Defence (MOD) recently initiated a major review of the kind of defence it needs to provide. It is called the Strategic Defence Review, and it spells out what needs changing if the Armed Forces are to adapt to the world in the 21st century.

Many of the measures recommended by the Review have already been put into practice and are busy shaping just what the Armed Forces will be like over the next few decades. For example, the idea of operating jointly has taken a huge step forward with the creation of a **Joint Rapid Reaction Force.** The pool of forces available will vary from time to time but its final approximate size and shape will include around 20 major warships (aircraft carriers, attack submarines, amphibious ships, destroyers or frigates), about 22 other vessels (mine warfare and support ships), 4 ground force brigades, about 110 combat aircraft and over 160 other aircraft. Relations with other nations – both allies and former enemies – are being strengthened, with more work being planned to help other countries bring their armed forces under full democratic control. And for the servicemen and -women themselves, the MOD is now doing more than ever to provide ongoing support for both them and their families – good news if you're planning to join up!

The Strategic Defence Review also underlines the role played by the reserve forces.

RESERVE FORCES

The UK also has substantial reserve forces – fully integrated and essential parts of the overall defence force that serves on a paid voluntary basis, usually part-time. They are:

- ▶ the Territorial Army – TA
- ▶ the Royal Naval Reserve – RNR (and the Royal Marines Reserve – RMR)
- ▶ the Royal Auxiliary Air Force – RAuxAF.

In all, there are around 48,000 members of the reserve forces, the majority serving in the TA. Far from being a hobby for 'weekend warriors', the reason for their existence is to provide fully trained personnel for operations all over the world, as and when required. Without them, the Armed Forces simply wouldn't be able to fulfil the kind of responsibilities outlined above.

It's often said that the reserves provide the best of both worlds, allowing the reservists to have both a civilian and military life and to enjoy the substantial crossover of skills and experience that results. If, after having read through the rest of this guide, you're not entirely sure whether you want to pursue a full-time career in the Armed Forces, but would still like to get involved and benefit from some of the training, then the reserve forces could well be the option for you.

DID YOU KNOW?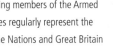

Serving members of the Armed Forces regularly represent the Home Nations and Great Britain at international sporting events – even the Olympics.

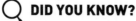

If you're too young, or not quite ready, to join either the regular forces or the reservists, then you can still get involved with the cadet forces – the Combined Cadet Force, the Sea Cadet Corps, the Army Cadet Force and the Air Training Corps.

THE CADETS

There are currently more than 44,000 cadets in the Army Cadet Force, 41,000 in the Air Cadet Organisation and 15,000 in the Sea Cadets. They all have access to excellent training as well as having the buzz of going on expeditions, many of which contribute towards the Duke of Edinburgh Award scheme. The cadet forces and corps provide not only an opportunity for you to have fun and keep fit but also a good way of developing the kind of leadership and team skills that will help you in adult life. They can prepare you, too, of course, for an eventual life in the Forces.

LIFE IN THE FORCES

All the various elements of the Armed Forces do vastly different work, but they all share one thing in common – the lifestyle – which can be challenging, rewarding, exciting, difficult, fun, pressured ... It's not your usual 9 to 5 job, and it's never easy – there's the training, both physical and mental; the travel; the time spent away from home; the regular moves; the responsibility; the unpredictability; the discipline of following orders and the potentially dangerous and traumatic experiences.

It's also never boring, providing varied opportunities and experiences that you'd never find in the civilian world. The training, while hard work, is some of the best in the world, allowing you to earn the kind of professional qualifications that will set you up for life. The sense of achievement that comes with being part of an organisation that's a force for good all around the world is also unrivalled.

But perhaps the most significant aspect of life in the Forces is the feeling of teamwork and camaraderie between the people who live, work and go through so much together. Whether playing football or learning to dive, building a house in war-torn Kosovo, spending months underwater cut off from the rest of civilisation, delivering humanitarian aid to the people of Mozambique, winding down at the end of the day or engaging the enemy on land, sea or in the air, it's the friendship and support of a close-knit team that members of the Armed Forces rely on to do their jobs.

DID YOU KNOW?

With bases in many countries throughout the world, the Armed Forces give you the chance to live as well as work abroad, to visit new places, to experience different cultures and meet new people.

Many people thrive on this kind of lifestyle; others don't suit it at all. You need to think very carefully about whether this is the right environment for you. One thing should be clear by now: the size and scope of the Armed Forces mean that the range of careers on offer is substantial to say the least. As the following chapters will reveal, it's not quite as simple as choosing the Army, Navy or Air Force, or saying that you 'want to fly planes' or 'be a Marine'.

CHAPTER 3
THE ARMY

QUICK FACTS

▶ There are more than 100,000 men and women in the regular British Army, supported by around 40,000 part-time, paid Volunteer Reservists of the Territorial Army (TA).

▶ There are more than 150 individual roles, or trades, available within the Army.

▶ The Army is committed to creating a diverse service, with equal opportunities for all.

▶ 70% of jobs in the Army are open to women as well as men. They exclude ground combat roles requiring levels of muscle strength apparently achieved by only around 1% of women.

▶ In 2005, there was a rise of 9.2% in the number of recruits joining the Army, but this figure still fell short of the overall target. Retention is still being addressed (*Defence News*, July 2008 issue).

WHAT'S IT ALL ABOUT?

In simple terms, the Army is the part of the Armed Forces that specialises in operating on the ground. One of the most highly trained and respected armies in the world, the British Army is almost unrivalled in its ability to provide a diverse range of services – from peacekeeping and helping the UK's civilian community to delivering humanitarian aid and fighting a war.

In more recent years, the Army has made significant contributions to United Nations, NATO and coalition forces in locations such as the Balkans, Afghanistan, Sierra Leone, Cyprus and Iraq. Alongside these commitments, the Army also has garrison forces stationed in Brunei, Cyprus, Germany, Gibraltar and the Falklands, as well as military teams and advisers posted in up to 25 countries worldwide. Like most organisations, the Army has a fairly rigid hierarchy – a structure that details who does what and who obeys whom in the chain of command.

CHAIN OF COMMAND

The most senior person in the British Army is the Chief of the General Staff, who reports to the government and is responsible for the overall management and fighting effectiveness of the service. Day-to-day management is the responsibility of the Army Board. Serving under the Board is a disciplined hierarchy of officers and soldiers who are responsible for distributing and delivering on the orders that come down from the top. In general, officers do the leading and managing, while soldiers focus on individual military roles or trades. Everyone, though, follows orders! The more senior the officer, the greater the number of people under his or her command, and hence the more responsibility he or she has. From the top down, the full rank structure for the Army is shown in Figures 2 and 3.

Command structure

You can choose to join the Army at either soldier or officer level, depending on your own particular ambitions, skills and qualifications. Of course, joining as a soldier doesn't stop you becoming an Officer in the future because, if you can demonstrate leadership potential and achieve the right qualifications, opportunities for promotion are plentiful. Similarly, joining as an officer doesn't mean that you'll be confined to a desk. The precise nature of your career will depend mainly on the regiment or corps you choose to join. If you are aged between 12 and 18 years, don't forget to find out more about

DID YOU KNOW?

Since a revolution took place in the country in 1948, Costa Rica has been the only Central American country without an army.

the Army Cadet Force, which will give you a taste of the Army. Membership means taking part in activities such as survival skills, shooting, orienteering, Duke of Edinburgh Award scheme, camping, obstacle courses and military tests.

How the Army is organised

The British Army is organised into an arrangement of divisions, brigades, regiments and battalions, corps and specialist units.

Divisions
Usually made up of three or four brigades. It may be a fighting formation, such as the 1st Armoured Division, or administrative

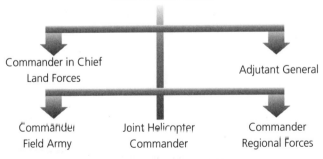

FIGURE 1
COMMAND STRUCTURE – ARMY

Chief of General Staff

Commander in Chief
Land Forces

Adjutant General

Commander
Field Army

Joint Helicopter
Commander

Commander
Regional Forces

FIGURE 2
COMMISSIONED OFFICERS

Field Marshall

↓

General

↓

Lieutenant General

↓

Major General

↓

Brigadier

↓

Colonel

↓

Lieutenant Colonel

↓

Major

↓

Captain

↓

Lieutenant

↓

Second Lieutenant

↓

Officer Designate

↓

Officer Cadet

FIGURE 3
NON-COMMISSIONED OFFICERS AND OTHER RANKS

Warrant Officer Class 1 (Regimental Sergeant Major)

Warrant Officer Class 2 (Quartermaster Sergeant)

Staff Sergeant or Colour Sergeant for some infantry regiments

Sergeant

Corporal or Bombardier for an artillery regiment

Lance Corporal or Lance Bombardier (artillery)

Private Soldier/Recruit

with responsibility for units in a particular geographical area.
When you 'join the Army' you actually have to choose a particular
regiment or corps.

Brigade
A collection of units and supporting elements, grouped together
for specific roles, usually numbering around 5,000 soldiers.

Specialist units
These are formed when specific demands cannot be met via the
usual structures or chains of command (e.g. Reserve Training and

Mobilisation Centre, UK Mines Information, and Training Centre and the Media Operations Group).

Regiments and Corps

A regiment usually contains around 650 soldiers who work to provide a particular service. Infantry and Royal Electrical and Mechanical Engineers (REME) regiments are divided into battalions of 650 soldiers.

DID YOU KNOW?

The Army's Royal Engineers took part in the very first FA Cup final in 1872. On that occasion they lost, but they were successful in 1875.

A corps is a branch of the Army that is responsible for a particular kind of work such as engineering or combat. There are 16 main regiments and corps, each one made up of a collection of further regiments and other groupings that share an area of interest or expertise.

- ▶ **Household Cavalry and Royal Armoured Corps (RAC)** – along with the combat element of the Household Cavalry, the RAC provides mobile firepower, e.g. tanks and other armoured vehicles.

- ▶ **Infantry** – just over one fifth of the Army; engages the enemy on the ground.

- ▶ **Army Air Corps** – the Army's own airborne capability.

- ▶ **Royal Regiment of Artillery** – provides indirect fire support and air defence in the field; literally, the 'big guns'!

- ▶ **Royal Engineers** – improves the Army's battlefield mobility whilst restricting the enemy's, e.g. by building and destroying bridges.

- ▶ **Royal Signals** – provides essential communication and electronic warfare support.

- ▶ **Royal Army Chaplains' Department** – provides chaplains of all denominations; responsible for moral and spiritual welfare of the troops.

- ▶ **Royal Logistic Corps (RLC)** – provides and distributes equipment and stores such as mail and food.

- ▶ **Royal Army Medical Corps** – provides healthcare both on the battlefield and for Army personnel and their families in peacetime.

- ▶ **Royal Electrical and Mechanical Engineers** – maintains all the Army's equipment, from helicopters to small firearms.

- ▶ **Adjutant General's Corps** – provides support in areas such as finance, administration, education, legal services and policing.

- ▶ **Royal Army Veterinary Corps** – cares for the Army's animals.

- ▶ **Royal Army Dental Corps** – cares for Army smiles, generally in dental centres, but might deploy to field units when needed.

- ▶ **Intelligence Corps** – a specialist range of analysts and linguists trained to anticipate threats to our security and know how to counter them.

- ▶ **Queen Alexandra's Royal Army Nursing Corps** – QARANC provides nursing support in both peace and war.

- ▶ **Corps of Army Music** – provides musicians for Army bands; supports the Army Medical Services during conflict.

By looking at the list of corps and their responsibilities, you should get a good idea of the range of different careers there are available.

CAREER GROUPS AND JOBS

If you're still not sure where you might fit in, the Army has been helpful enough to summarise what's on offer in a selection of career groups based on civilian rather than military terminology.

- ▶ **Combat** – providing capability in front-line fighting. Jobs include infantry soldier; tank crewman; gunner; aviation groundcrew specialist.

- ▶ **Engineering** – maintaining equipment, building structures. Technical problem solving and fixing. Jobs include armourer; combat engineer; carpenter and joiner; bricklayer and concreter; aircraft technician; electrician; design draughtsman; vehicle mechanic; radio systems operator; heating and plumbing engineer; geographic data technician; metalsmith.

▶ **IT and Communications** – building technological and communications networks. Jobs include signals electrician; systems engineer technician; radio systems operator; military operator; electronics technician.

▶ **Logistics** – transport and supply specialists delivering food, fuel, ammunition, vehicles and other equipment. Jobs include ammunition technician; driver; port operator; seaman; supply specialist; supply controller; chef; movement controller.

▶ **Healthcare** – ensures the health and strength of personnel and animals. Jobs include combat medical technician; nurse; dental technician; veterinary technician; radiographer; biomedical scientist; clinical physiologists; pharmacy technician; and veterinary roles.

▶ **Human Resources, Administration and Finance** – maintaining the smooth running and effectiveness of the Army, including payment of salaries and welfare. Jobs include military clerk.

▶ **Specialist** – providing highly specialised capabilities such as policing, dog training, playing in a band, etc. Jobs include musician; linguist; farrier; royal military police; mounted gunner; dog trainer.

▶ **Officer** – leading, managing, organising and motivating teams of skilled people across a range of occupational areas, as well as providing additional capabilities. Jobs include army chaplain; army legal services; medical officer; intelligence officer; veterinary officer; infantry platoon commander; personnel officer; tank commander.

If you're still at school, there are a number of ways in which you can continue your education with the Army. See the chapter on Training (Chapter 11).

CHAPTER 4
REAL LIVES – THE ARMY

BRIGADIER STACEY TAYLOR

Stacey is 26 years old and currently serving with 3rd Regiment Royal Horse Artillery. Her main duty in the Regiment is working as the 2IC (Second in Command) for C Battery in the Battery Quartermaster Stores (BQMS).

Stacey says:

'The Cadet Force had a major impact on me when I was young, and was my main reason for joining the Army. I just loved everything about it; from getting dirty to sleeping out in the woods. When I was 16, I signed up and joined the Army.

I joined the Gunners because in the Cadets we visited a lot of different ACFs around the North West and we attended quite a few Liverpool shows. I just loved the AS90 – the big guns, that's what I called them at the time. From then I was hooked and just had to join the Artillery.'

What she enjoys most about her role is that her life has completely changed. As she joined so young, she has had to grow up very fast and make decisions for herself.

'I meet fantastic people every day and get to travel to places I never thought possible. That's why I love my job so much; you couldn't ask for a better way of life.'

She has also made her family very proud.

'I grew up in a very rough part of Liverpool called Kensington, where everybody knows each other's business.'

She affirms:

'I have now served 10 years to the day and I still enjoy it (that's the truth). I completed my training at two different training depots. Firstly, Phase 1 training which was 15 weeks long at ATR Pirbright and, once that was complete (which was the proudest day of my life), I moved onto Larkhill for my trade training, where I learned what I was going to do when I arrived at my regiment. I spent three months at Larkhill doing my basic signals course and then completed my Cat B driving licence. It was great being able to drive a car at 17 years old.'

In September 1999, she moved over to Germany and joined 3rd Regiment Royal Horse Artillery. 'I was very nervous,' she states. She has taken part in many exercises to Poland, Germany, UK, Canada and Kenya. She has completed operational tours in Kosovo, Op Telic 1, a UN tour of Cyprus and Op Telic 7. Each operation is given a randomly assigned code name, and will have a number assigned to it, depending on which deployment you are on. Therefore 'Operation Telic' was the code name given to the Iraq conflict, so, for example, Op Telic 1 was the initial invasion.

'A career in the Army has given me a great opportunity to do something for my country, making me proud of myself. My greatest achievement so far has to be getting to the rank of Brigadier as a female in a male-oriented environment.'

Qualifications she has gained since being in the Army are CLM, which is Numeracy and Literacy Level 2, and also an NVQ in Telecommunications.

'My ambition in the Army is to be the first female Regimental Sergeant Major (RSM). As a female in the Army you have a great opportunity to show that females can do the same job as males in some areas. We deserve a chance to prove ourselves and what we can be within the Armed Forces.'

OFFICER CADET GEORGE HUXFORD

George is 22 years old and in the process of applying for entry to Sandhurst.

After completing three years at Sussex University, George had a 2:1 in Product Design, but was finding it hard to get work. He had applied to several graduate training schemes but nothing was really offering either the salary he wanted or the opportunities. George's family has a strong Army background: his dad was in the TA until this year; his uncle started as a soldier and progressed to officer before getting a job with NATO. This meant he had a greater knowledge of the job than others and was able to weigh up the pros and cons. He is the fifth George Huxford consecutively applying to the services.

George's year of working in retail since leaving university was beginning to get him down; a life in a low-paid, low-reward job seemed to be beckoning and he didn't want his degree or skills to go to waste. George felt that he had missed out on a lot of jobs, as the first stage was often a series of impersonal online tests, during which he felt he couldn't put his true self across; and his dyslexia didn't help with online essays and comprehension tests. At the AOSB (Army Officer Selection Board) he had to do a few tests, but his dyslexia isn't considered to be a problem – the whole individual is considered.

He decided to visit his local Army recruitment office and after an interview and a two-day briefing he subsequently went on an open day with the Royal Engineers, who offered him a sponsorship. With this encouragement, George will begin the intense mental and physical training programme required to gain entry to the officer training at Sandhurst. Despite the intensity of the final AOSB and all the subsequent interviews and tests, George enjoyed the fast-paced environment and the chance to socialise with other people with similar interests.

'I'm really looking forward to starting at Sandhurst and the chance to go on loads of adventurous training. The opportunity to go snowboarding, skydiving and whatever else I can think of and be paid for it, it is going to be great! And at the end of it I get to do a really important and worthwhile job.'

CHAPTER 5
THE ROYAL NAVY

QUICK FACTS

▶ The Navy has over 80 ships, ranging in size from aircraft carriers to patrol boats. It also has around 200 aircraft and over 50 support/training aircraft, plus a submarine force.

▶ In all, there are 43,000 personnel in the Navy, with 50 recruits joining the Royal Marines every two weeks.

▶ Women serve in all classes of surface warships and ashore, but are restricted from operating and fighting in front-line infantry units, so are unable to join the Royal Marines, the Submarine Service and Mine Clearance Diving.

▶ There are many and varied opportunities for civilians working in direct support to uniformed personnel.

WHAT'S IT ALL ABOUT?

The Royal Navy plays a major role in the defence of our country's interests and many international peacekeeping and humanitarian operations. It has been a major player in the fortunes of the UK for many hundreds of years, since long before the invention of air travel. This is hardly surprising in what is, after all, an island nation whose seas are both a national border and a trade route to almost anywhere else on the planet. Indeed, more than 90% of the imports and exports that the UK relies on for generating much

27

of its wealth are still transported by sea, making the Royal Navy and the Merchant Navy just as relevant now as they ever have been. Seaborne trade is forecast to increase substantially by 2015. For more information on the Merchant Navy, see the Further Information chapter in this book for contact details.

A versatile force, the Navy spans land and air as well as sea. It has its own ships, submarines, aircraft and commandos (the Royal Marines), which can be used collectively to provide a full service or to work alongside the Army, Royal Air Force and other allied forces. Perhaps its key capability in this respect is the way it can be deployed rapidly to do a job almost anywhere in the world and then remain there until it's no longer needed.

For example, the Navy has in recent times been involved in a wide range of activities, including conflicts and peacekeeping in Afghanistan, Sierra Leone and Iraq; enforcing UN trade sanctions in the Gulf; providing humanitarian relief in the Caribbean and Mozambique; patrolling fishing grounds and ocean oilfields or other waters to prevent illegal activities such as drug trafficking; searching for and rescuing people stranded at sea; and evacuating British citizens from trouble spots such as Albania and Indonesia.

In addition to such roles, the Navy also has the unique, special responsibility of providing the UK's continuous nuclear deterrent through its Vanguard-class submarines and Trident missiles. Fully committed to NATO, this is a force for European and international stability.

As in the Army, there is a complex chain of command.

CHAIN OF COMMAND

At the top of the Navy tree sits the Chief of Staff, who has ultimate responsibility for putting the naval aspect of defence policy into

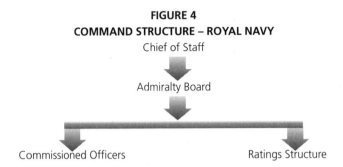

FIGURE 4
COMMAND STRUCTURE – ROYAL NAVY

Chief of Staff

Admiralty Board

Commissioned Officers   Ratings Structure

practice efficiently and effectively. Then there is the Admiralty Board. Then there is a hierarchy of officers and 'ratings', the naval equivalent of soldiers. Ratings serve on ships or on shore supporting the sea-going fleet and personnel. They serve under officers who are trained to perform key specialist operational roles as well as having management responsibilities.

You can join the Royal Navy at both rating and officer levels. To be an officer you need certain minimum academic qualifications, but don't worry if you don't have them at the moment because you can study for them while you're a rating. You also need the potential to lead. If you have this and the academic ability, there are opportunities to become a commissioned officer. If you are 13 or in Year 9 at school, or have not reached your 20th birthday, don't forget to find out more about the Sea Cadets. You will experience a taste of life in the Navy. Membership means taking part in water-based activities, such as sailing, canoeing and rowing, and land-based activities, such as rock climbing, shooting, cookery and music.

DID YOU KNOW?

One in five serving Naval Officers joined the Navy as an Ordinary Rating, proving that if you can demonstrate that you have what it takes you can make progress up the promotion ladder.

FIGURE 5
COMMISSIONED OFFICER STRUCTURE

Captain

Commander

Lieutenant Commander

Lieutenant

Sub-Lieutenant

FIGURE 6
RATINGS STRUCTURE

Warrant Officer 1

Chief Petty Officer

Petty Officer

Leading Hand

Royal Navy/Royal Marines Ratings

THE FLEET

The Royal Navy has a balanced force of more than 120 ships. The capability of this fleet is built around three key areas.

▶ **Carrier-borne aircraft** – provides the ability to control the air as well as the sea, and to project power inland, taking off from three Invincible-class aircraft carriers.

▶ **Nuclear-powered submarines** – able to cover long distances at high speed without refuelling and remain submerged for long periods, vital qualities for long-range, stealthy operations.

▶ **Amphibious forces** – help to deploy forces rapidly around the world by using specialist amphibious ships to land troops and firepower directly from the sea and straight into action.

The rest of the fleet is built around these elements and is made up of the following kinds of vessel:

▶ **Frigates and Destroyers** – the workhorses of the fleet, protecting friendly forces from attack as well as seeking out and destroying the enemy. In peacetime, they are used for such tasks as peacekeeping, humanitarian aid, guard ship duties and enforcing sanctions.

▶ **Mine Countermeasures Vessels** – painstakingly use hi-tech equipment and the skills of the ships' seamen and -women to clear seas of mines, making them safe for other boats and ships.

▶ **Royal Fleet Auxiliary** – specialist ships that make sure that warships remain supplied with fuel, ammunition, food and other stores. They are also used to bring aid to crisis-hit locations all over the world.

▶ **Fishery Protection and Patrol Vessels** – protect stocks of fish by enforcing UK and European fishery regulations 365 days a year. They also patrol oilfields and other important areas.

> ▶ **Hydrographic Flotilla** – continues the Royal Navy's long tradition of charting the oceans and coastlines of the world, refining and updating Admiralty charts used the world over.

> ▶ **Search and Rescue** – all naval ships and aircraft can carry out this task when necessary, but there are also specialist squadrons that operate out of Cornwall and Ayrshire.

Once again, it's easy to see that the Navy offers a wide variety of roles and opportunities.

CAREER GROUPS AND JOBS

DID YOU KNOW?

The Royal Navy has its own parachute display team, known as 'The Raiders'.

There are a number of areas and roles that you can work in as part of the Royal Navy, catering for all kinds of interests and abilities. If you decide that you do want to join up, you will also have to choose one of these specialisations, which are organised according to six career groups that correspond to the six branches of the Navy.

> ▶ **Warfare** – operating and maintaining the ship and submarine weapons systems, gathering and coordinating information, and helping to guide the weapons to their targets. Jobs include communications technician; diver; operator mechanic; warfare officer.

> ▶ **Submarines** – providing front-line, 24-hour protection, cruising the world beneath the surface of the ocean, sometimes for as long as three months at a time. Jobs include operator mechanic; caterer; marine engineering mechanic; submarine warfare officer.

> ▶ **Air** – running the Navy's airborne capability. Jobs include naval airman; aircrew officer; air traffic controller.

> ▶ **Engineering** – ensuring all the vessels, weapons systems, aircraft and other equipment run smoothly. Jobs include engineering technician (artificer); air engineering technician;

marine engineering mechanic; engineer officer; information systems officer.

- ▶ **Supply/Services** – planning and delivering supplies and stores for time spent at sea, including food, usually months in advance. Jobs include caterer (chef); writer (administrative and accounting staff); steward; stores accountant; supply officer.

- ▶ **Medical** – caring for the sick and injured and maintaining the overall health of the fleet. Jobs include dental hygienist; medical assistant; dental surgery assistant; naval nurse; nursing officer; medical officer; dental officer.

The Navy also has its own special 'infantry' – the Royal Marine Corps.

THE ROYAL MARINES

The Royal Marine Corps is the Navy's very own 'infantry'. Operating at the sharp end, the Royal Marine Commandos – whose motto, *'per mare per terram'*, means 'by sea, by land' – are usually the first (or sometimes the only) force into battle, deployed directly from amphibious landing craft and often engaging in highly specialised activities such as jungle and mountain warfare. As such, they need to be among the most focused, ruthless and highly trained people in the whole of the Armed Forces.

The Corps is characterised by a 'no compromise' approach to training, exercises and operations. It is committed to excellence, almost to the point of being fanatical, maintaining its standards by putting recruits through the most demanding training course in the British Armed Forces. The

DID YOU KNOW?

The British Royal Fleet Auxiliary ship RFA *Argus* would be a hospital ship were it not for its armaments, which, under the Geneva Convention prevents it from being officially known as a floating hospital.

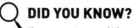

DID YOU KNOW?

The extreme nature of life and training in the Marines means that entry is only open to men, except for the positions of musician and bugler within the Royal Marines Band Service, which are open to both men and women.

famous green berets that new Commandos are awarded on completion of initial training are a symbol of the kind of dedication, technical ability, physical fitness, discipline, self-confidence and initiative it takes to become a member of this elite team.

Like the rest of the Royal Navy, the Marines provide you with a range of possible specialisations after you have passed your training – from electronic warfare and illustrator to physical training instructor to general duties – as well as the opportunity to become a Royal Marines Officer. You can even combine a military role with a love and talent for music by joining the Royal Marines Band Service – an outfit you might be familiar with if you have ever watched the FA Cup final!

CHAPTER 6
REAL LIVES – THE ROYAL NAVY

AIR ENGINEERING TECHNICIAN THOMAS BEST

In civilian life, Thomas Best worked as an apprentice vehicle technician for Audi. Now, he's an Air Engineering Technician with the Fleet Air Arm, looking after Lynx helicopters at the Yeovilton Royal Naval Air Station in Somerset.

'I was 19 years old when I joined the Royal Navy, which seemed like the right time for me. My application process was extremely fast: from completing my interview, medical and fitness test to joining HMS *Raleigh* for basic training only took 2 months. I signed a contract for 18.5 years and I've still got 16 left to serve; however, I can submit my notice to leave the Service at any time. But I absolutely love my job, and to be honest, the time is going by far too fast.

During basic training, you're taught to work as a team. Throughout your course, you're pushed to your mental and physical limits. You have to be fit: over the nine weeks you're marching, shooting, swimming, doing obstacle and assault courses, tramping across Dartmoor and training in firefighting and ship damage repair.

You also get to go to sea and experience life on a warship. You live in a Mess Deck, which typically comprises a sleeping area and living/social area. It's very comfortable, if a little cramped, but it just adds to the adventure of being at sea!

Most of all, though, basic training is about making new friends. The best thing you'll have in the Royal Navy are your workmates and friends. We're all a family in the Fleet Air Arm and look after each other.

Once I'd completed Phase 1 Training HMS *Raleigh*, I went on to Phase 2 training at HMS *Sultan* in Gosport, to become an Air Engineering Technician, or AET. About halfway through, you're given an opportunity to choose a specific aircraft type, and I picked Lynx helicopters.

As an AET, I'm involved in maintaining the aircraft: servicing it before and after the flight and also carrying out routine tasks such as regular checks on the engine, hydraulics or fuel systems. I find it fascinating and I love working in the aviation environment. A Lynx crew is very small – only 10 people – and even though I'm in the Engineering branch, as opposed to being a Pilot or Observer, I work alongside Aircrew day in, day out. I also get loads of opportunities to fly in the helos I work with!

In this job, I'm permanently based ashore, and will only go to sea for 6–9 months every 2.5 years. I haven't been lucky enough to go away on a deployment yet, so in terms of being away from my family, I couldn't really say how I'm going to find it. The longest I've been away from home so far is when I spent three weeks on an aircraft carrier, HMS *Ark Royal*. I must admit it I did get lost quite a bit, due to the sheer size of the ship and the number of passageways. It was hard work but great fun!

Working with the Lynx, the only time I'll get to go away is when the aircraft is embarked on a frigate or destroyer. If you're a Sea King or Merlin helicopter specialist, you'll be either on carriers or HMS *Ocean*, which is an amphibious assault ship: as a Harrier AET, you will just go to the carriers. I'll always have a say in where I go, but ultimately the needs of the Royal Navy will dictate where I end up.

I've signed up for a Full Career of 18.5 years, but my personal ambitions mean I might be serving for a different length of time. I'm a Commission and Warrant (CW) candidate, which means although I joined the Royal Navy as a rating, I've shown the aptitude and determination to be selected for the Admiralty Interview Board and potentially become an officer in the future.

I know it's a cliché, but the Royal Navy isn't a job, it's a way of life. I took a little while to get used to the military way of doing things, but since joining I haven't looked back and I've loved every minute. What's been my best experience so far? It's been so packed I wouldn't know where to begin. I've been in flight simulators, flown in both fixed and rotary winged aircraft, joined loads of sports clubs and managed to get on the Black Cats helicopter display team. Compared to my previous life outside the Royal Navy, I have far more opportunities for sport, travel, education, meeting new friends and career stability. It's all made me a much more confident person.

We all join the Royal Navy knowing we could go into an area of conflict. And if we're not on deployment, we're training for it, or carrying out Maritime Security Operations. The job requires us to be away for periods of anything from one week to six months, but dealing with separation gets easier with experience. The Royal Navy has a great support network for families at home and does everything it can to keep us in contact with our loved ones, with satellite phones, email and, of course, letters.

The job is fantastic and takes us to places we'd never get to visit in civilian life. And, unlike a lot of people, when we say we "work hard and play hard", we really mean it!'

LOGISTICS OFFICER MARK TOOGOOD

Lieutenant Mark Toogood joined the Royal Navy in 1991 as a Chef. In 2000, he qualified as a Physical Training Instructor (PTI), serving both at sea and at the Royal Navy School of Physical Training at HMS *Temeraire* in Hampshire. In 2007, he attended the Admiralty Interview Board and was selected for Officer training. He passed out from Britannia Royal Naval College in April 2008, and is now on the Initial Logistics Officer Course at HMS *Raleigh* in Cornwall.

'I had my own, rather unusual reason for joining the Royal Navy: cricket! I wanted to be a pro, but finally I had to accept I would never be good enough. In the Navy, however, I knew I'd be able to play at a pretty high level by representing the Service, while pursuing a "proper" career.

So in 1991, I joined as a Chef, which is much like being a chef in civilian life, except it can be a lot more exciting! During my time on HMS *Cumberland*, for example, I spent nine months in the Northern Arabian Gulf and served as part of the Ship's Boarding Party, identifying and detaining Iraqi embargo busters. And in case you're wondering: yes, even sailors suffer from seasickness. It gets better the more time you spend at sea, but trust me, the first time I went on board ship I was as sick as a dog…

In 2000, I went back to my sporting roots and qualified as a Physical Training Instructor (PTI). I served on HMS *Iron Duke*, which is a Type 23 frigate, then became a Staff Instructor at the Royal Navy School of Physical Training at HMS *Temeraire* in Hampshire.

After seven years, I decided I was ready to take my career to the next level and attended the Admiralty Interview Board (AIB). Held at HMS *Sultan* in Hampshire, this is a three-day selection course for potential officers, consisting of physical, academic and leadership exercises and a formal interview. I was selected and passed out of Britannia Naval College as a Logistics Officer in April 2008.

Being a Logistician is a diverse and rewarding role, often described as 'the art of the impossible'. It's our job to ensure that everyone in the Royal Navy – all 37,000 of them – has exactly what they need to do their job, when they need it, wherever they are in the world.

As you might imagine, then, it's a busy life, whether you're an administrator in an Admiral's outer office, getting supplies to a warship on the other side of the world, or managing your department's personnel. As with all jobs, there are routine elements, but overall it's challenging, rewarding and sometimes very exciting. On a warship, you could act as Damage Control Officer when the ship goes into action; in the Gulf or the West Indies, you could be in command of a boarding party identifying and boarding vessels of interest. Plus, there's a plethora of 'out of branch' jobs.

As I've matured, I've come to realise that the Royal Navy is a fantastic employer. I've travelled to some amazing places – Florida, the Caribbean, South Africa, Goa, the Gulf, Rio de Janeiro – and taken part in important and rewarding deployments. Most importantly, I'm still having great fun. It's like having a large number of flatmates: when you share a living space, you form significant bonds with people. These, along with your shared experiences – good and bad – will bind you together for life. I'm very lucky in that I also have a phenomenal wife who supports everything I do, be it here in the UK or deployed overseas.

But have I fulfilled my cricketing ambitions? Absolutely. I went on my first tour in 1993 – to Barbados! – and since then I've played in South Africa and India. I'm delighted to say I'm still opening the batting for the Royal Navy; even better, playing representative sport is considered a 'duty commitment', so it doesn't come out of my annual leave!

I admit my motivation for joining was slightly unorthodox and I'd emphasise that the Royal Navy isn't a career decision to be taken lightly. What I can absolutely guarantee is that you'll have a great time with many opportunities!'

CHAPTER 7
THE ROYAL AIR FORCE

QUICK FACTS

▶ The Royal Air Force (RAF) has around 55 squadrons based in the UK and abroad.

▶ There are more than 50 types of job role on offer. There are great opportunities for those with a couple of GCSEs right up to graduate level. With the exception of the RAF Regiment, all RAF jobs are open to women – that's 96% of the total, and includes flying combat aircraft and support helicopters.

▶ The RAF employs and values people from all faith communities.

WHAT'S IT ALL ABOUT?

The job of the RAF is to deliver the UK Defence Vision which has three aims:

1. Defend the UK and its interests.
2. Strengthen international peace and stability.
3. Be a force for good in the world.

The RAF must be ready to deliver flexible air power anywhere in the world, responding swiftly and effectively to new threats and challenges. In terms of warfare, this usually means taking part in the first stage of a conflict, undermining the enemy's ability to make

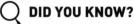

DID YOU KNOW?

In the Armed Forces you get the job you deserve. You don't necessarily have to join the ladder on the lowest rung, and you don't have to work your way through every junior rank before applying to train as an officer

war through precise bombing of strategic targets. It plays a key role in peacekeeping operations by helping to police the skies and enforce no-fly zones over trouble spots. It is also in an unrivalled position to move quickly and deliver disaster relief and other humanitarian aid, particularly to remote areas, both at home and abroad. Operating out of working stations all over the UK, it plays an active role in defending our own airspace as well as providing search and rescue services in and around the country's mountains and coastline.

In keeping with the general growth in joint operations, the RAF works increasingly closely with the Army and Navy in delivering these services. This includes delivering relief to flood-hit Mozambique, evacuation tasks, patrolling airspace over the Balkans, taking part in the coalition action against Iraq, building a school in Afghanistan and organising charitable appeals, such as 'Taking Football to Africa and Beyond'. This global appeal has involved distributing 12,000 tons of football kit and over 6,000 shirts to recipients in 22 countries.

The role of the RAF at home

At home, the role of the RAF is to defend the UK airspace. They are involved in search and rescue activities over both land and sea, community and conservation work, activities with schools and youth leadership courses. They also participate in ceremonial events, and you may have been lucky enough to have seen the famous aerobatics display team, the Red Arrows. If you are aged between 13 and 18, don't forget to find out more about the Air Training Corps, which will give you a taste of life in the Armed Services. Membership means taking part in activities such as camping here and abroad, first aid, adventure training and sports. RAF maths and science workshops are run in schools throughout the country, and if you are studying for a degree you can join University Air Squadrons. The RAF also sponsors sixth-formers wanting to become Officers.

DID YOU KNOW?

Other than Americans, the only people allowed to fly the F117 Stealth Fighter are highly trained RAF pilots.

Collectively, the RAF is a diverse team of highly organised and skilled individuals working closely together to deliver the required capability. As in the Army and Navy there is an organisational hierarchy.

CHAIN OF COMMAND

Just like the other Armed Forces, the RAF has a management structure and a hierarchy of ranks to provide a clear line of management.

At the top is the First Commander in Chief Air Command (CINC AIR) and the Air Force Board. He has two Deputies, both Air

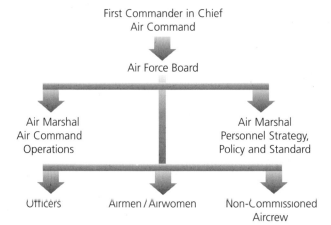

FIGURE 7
COMMAND STRUCTURE – RAF

First Commander in Chief
Air Command

Air Force Board

Air Marshal
Air Command
Operations

Air Marshal
Personnel Strategy,
Policy and Standard

Officers

Airmen / Airwomen

Non-Commissioned
Aircrew

Marshals, who have responsibilities which include Personnel Strategy, Policy and Standards, and Air Command Operations.

Officers

Officers are senior managers, and when you complete your officer training, you receive a 'commission' from the Queen which entitles you to give orders on behalf of the Crown.

The rank structure for officers is shown in Figure 8 (most senior first).

**FIGURE 8
OFFICERS**

Air Commodore

Group Captain

Wing Commander

Squadron Leader

Flight Lieutenant

Flying Officer

Pilot Officer

Airmen and airwomen

These personnel form the majority, and they work in ground support roles using specialist skills. If you want to, you can apply for a commission later in your career.

The rank structure is shown in Figure 9 (most senior first).

FIGURE 9
AIRMEN AND AIRWOMEN

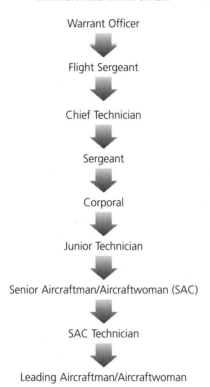

Warrant Officer

Flight Sergeant

Chief Technician

Sergeant

Corporal

Junior Technician

Senior Aircraftman/Aircraftwoman (SAC)

SAC Technician

Leading Aircraftman/Aircraftwoman

Non-Commissioned Aircrew (NC Aircrew)

Other staff have flying roles, such as weapon systems operator.
Their ranking is shown in Figure 10 (most senior first).

FIGURE 10
NON-COMMISSIONED AIRCREW (NC AIRCREW)

Master Aircrew

Flight Sergeant

Sergeant (Aircrew)

HQ AIR COMMAND

The RAF's Air Command is based at RAF High Wycombe, at Naphill in Buckinghamshire. The creation of a single command (there used to be three) in 2007 means that with one HQ, the RAF can provide a Coordinated air focus to other services (e.g. Ministry of Defence). Air Command is divided into 'groups' and then into 'wings'. These are put together from two or more squadrons – the basic organisational units of the RAF.

RAF BASES

There are 23 bases or 'stations' across the UK, including Northern Ireland, and each base has its own role, as part of Air Command. The largest base is Brize Norton. Bases are home to a number of squadrons, and are like small towns with their own shops, gyms, cinemas, banks, post offices, etc. They are usually situated away from the general public due to the noise of the aircraft, but are often within reach of big cities.

ABOUT THE AIRCRAFT

The Typhoon F2 (Eurofighter) is a combat aircraft, equipped with short-, medium- and long-range missiles and an advanced radar system, able to track multiple targets at long range.

The Tornado GR4 is the latest version of the primary attack aircraft, able to fly at low levels and exceed twice the speed of sound. It is equipped with laser and guided missiles, and its reconnaissance pod can image targets from a distance.

DID YOU KNOW?

A Tristar air-to-air refuelling aircraft dispenses up to 85,465 litres of fuel on a single sortie – enough for an average car to drive around the world three times.

The Merlin HC3 is also armed, and is the most up-to-date helicopter, able to carry 24 people and refuel in mid-air.

The Nimrod MRA4 is soon to replace the entire Nimrod fleet. It is the most advanced surveillance aircraft in the world.

Other aircraft include planes such as VC10s, Tristars, Sentinel, Harrier GR9 and other types of helicopter such as Chinook, Puma and Sea King.

This overview makes it clear there's a lot more variety on offer in the RAF than simply flying aircraft; we'll look at the full range of roles below.

CAREER GROUPS AND JOBS

When you mention the possibility of a career in the Air Force, thoughts usually turn immediately to the aircrews – the teams of people responsible for flying and operating the kinds of aircraft just mentioned. However, there are many more people who provide the essential support that's necessary to deliver the RAF's air power – from those who control the communications links between the air and ground to those who keep the aircraft in working order.

When considering jobs in the RAF, it's helpful to split them into groups. Under each group, a range of ranks and jobs are listed which may interest you and provide a base for your further research.

▶ **Logistics and equipment** – driver; mover; supplier; supply officer.

▶ **Medical and medical support** – biomedical scientist; dental nurse; dental officer; dental technician; environmental health technician; medical officer; medical support officer; nursing officer.

▶ **Personnel support** – administrative officer; chaplain; legal officer; musician; personnel administrator; physical education officer; physical training instructor; training officer.

▶ **Force protection** – firefighter; RAF police; RAF police officer; RAF regiment gunner; RAF regiment officer.

▶ **Engineering and technical** – aircraft technician; engineer officer; general technician; survival equipment fitter; weapon technician.

▶ **Air operations support** – aerospace systems operator; air cartographer; flight operations assistant/officer; air traffic control officer.

▶ **Aircrew** – pilot; weapon systems officer; weapon systems operator (acoustic); weapon systems operator (crew men).

▶ **Catering and hospitality** – caterer; catering officer; chef.

▶ **Communications and intelligence** – aerial erector; ICT specialist; intelligence analyst (voice); intelligence officer; photographer.

DID YOU KNOW?

The RAF always tries to let married couples work at the same base or at nearby bases. And for airmen and -women on an overseas posting, it does its best to support partners until their return.

You need to consider exactly what it means to be in the Armed Forces in the 21st century. One third of all RAF personnel are engineering and technical specialists. There are 20 types of specialist officer roles listed below in alphabetical order, so you should be able to find one to suit your skills and ambitions:

- administrative officer
- aerospace battle manager
- air traffic control officer
- catering officer
- chaplain
- dental officer
- engineer officer
- flight operations officer
- intelligence officer
- legal officer
- medical officer
- medical support officer
- nursing officer
- physical education officer
- pilot
- RAF police officer
- RAF regiment officer
- supply officer
- training officer
- weapon systems officer.

CHAPTER 8
REAL LIVES – THE ROYAL AIR FORCE

RAF ENGINEER OFFICER KARIM HOMSEY

RAF Coningsby

Life is magic for Flight Lieutenant Homsey. Working with state-of-the-art technology on the Typhoon aircraft, RAF Engineer Officer Karim Homsey is based at RAF Coningsby, working on the Typhoon Operation Evaluation Unit. When not working, Karim gets up to all sorts of tricks as the resident magician.

With a passion for all things aviation and an aversion to working 9 to 5, Karim Homsey knew that he wanted a career with a difference. Whilst studying for a degree in aerospace engineering at Manchester University, Karim assessed his options and pursued an application with the RAF. With previous experience as an Air Cadet, Karim was familiar with the military lifestyle and was confident that a career as an Engineer Officer was the right choice for him. He explains:

'I had always been interested in the RAF and as a teenager enjoyed being an Air Cadet. With an aptitude for engineering-based subjects it made sense to apply for a job that suited my abilities. I also like the idea of being, in part, responsible for the airworthiness of aircraft.'

After graduating from Initial Officer Training at RAF Cranwell in Lincolnshire, Karim stayed at that base and began the specialist engineer training that all Engineer Officers in the RAF must complete. He reveals:

'Whilst I felt relatively at home with the initial officer training, possibly due to my time in the Air Cadets, the specialist training was a further challenge. There were plenty of exercises and theory, resulting in an exam per week on subjects that were different to what I had studied at university.'

First posted to RAF Brize Norton, as Officer Commanding General Engineering Flight, Karim was immediately in charge of 75 personnel and a wide range of equipment.

'In my first posting I experienced a section ramping up to 24-hour manning at short notice, a situation many of my personnel hadn't witnessed before. It was frantic, preparing equipment for deployment to the Gulf and everyone worked extremely hard to get the job done. That lasted for a few weeks before we resumed normal hours.'

Karim's second posting was to RAF Marham, where he worked on Tornado GR4 aircraft and says:

'Getting posted to 13 Squadron was a dream come true, as this was the job I had joined up to do. I was responsible for the airworthiness of the Squadron's aircraft and their associated weapons systems. When on operations, the technicians would come to me for authority to maintain aircraft that were armed. It was up to me to decide if it was safe to work on them, or if the weapons needed to be removed first.'

Whist at RAF Marham Karim spent approximately a third of his time on exercises and operational detachments. From Canada to Kuwait,

Turkey and Qatar, Karim's job has taken him to some far-flung places and provided experiences not easily rivalled. He explains:

'In September 2004 I went to Qatar on Op Telic (Iraq) and it was hard for everyone. As the Squadron Engineering Officer, I worked extremely long hours without a day off during the whole detachment. That is balanced, though, by opportunities like the one I had in Nevada, where I was able to explore Las Vegas and see a world-class magic show.'

Karim's third posting was to RAF Wyton, where he was the engineering authority responsible for the airworthiness of the airframe for the Tornado F3 and GR4 fleet. The role was about preserving the working life of the aircraft structure and its component parts. He explains:

'My role at RAF Wyton was busy and interesting. Day to day I was making decisions that affected anything from individual aircraft to the whole fleet, taking advice from industry but ultimately making the decisions. I chaired a Tri-Nation meeting, during which we investigated various aspects from individual panel repairs to assessing structural fatigue in order to determine the best solutions for the partner nations.'

Currently based at RAF Coningsby, working on the RAF's most modern combat aircraft, the Typhoon, Karim has landed another prime catch. He admits:

'As the Trials Engineering Officer on 17 (Reserve) Squadron, the Typhoon Operation Evaluation Unit (OEU), I am involved in developing the aircraft's future capability.

Ever since I was at university I have been interested in flight testing and the OEU is at the cutting edge of the RAF's technology. In May 2008 I will be running the detachment for the flight trials taking place in the US. The rest of the Typhoon Force eagerly awaits the results of all our flight trials; once we prove a new aircraft system and procedures are safe, these are implemented by the front line.'

Outside of work Karim likes to get up to all sorts of tricks. With years of practice performing magic tricks, Karim has perfected the art of illusion and enjoys wowing crowds at RAF and civilian functions. He reveals:

'I was five when I did my first magic trick, and then at secondary school I found a friend who was also interested in magic. We would bounce ideas off one another or swap tricks and to this day still do.

At times, having the odd trick up my sleeve has come in handy. For example, when I went for a university interview and the professor asked me what my interests were I made a pack of cards disappear right in front of his eyes. He couldn't work out how I had done it but it must have impressed him as he mentioned it in my offer of a place.'

Summing up the benefits of being an engineer in the RAF, Karim concludes:

'I never get bored because my job changes every couple of years and for me the lifestyle and opportunity to travel are amazing. I enjoy the sport and adventure training as well as the general social scene that comes with working in such a close-knit environment. Professionally I also value working with people who take pride in their work and are focused on the task in hand. I certainly think I made the right decision in joining the RAF to pursue a career in engineering.'

Pay after training: £28,950

Joining age: 21–36

Usual service: 6 years

Open to: men or women

PERSONNEL ADMINISTRATOR CORPORAL KRISTAL HARDY

Corporal Kristal Hardy is a PA with a difference. Working as a Personnel Administrator in the Royal Air Force, Kristal has faced a variety of challenges, including a recent four-month detachment to Afghanistan. Prior to that she was PA to the Station Commander based at RAF Gibraltar. Her 10 years of experience is now being utilised to help others: when she begins a new post at the MOD School of Personnel Administration she will be an NVQ Assessor.

The daughter of military parents, and an Air Cadet herself, Kristal was familiar with the RAF way of life and was adamant she wanted to join up at the first available opportunity. Keen on a customer-focused career she was selected to train as a Personnel Administrator and took to it like a duck to water. Kristal explains:

'After initial basic and trade training I thought I was well prepared for the job, so at my first posting at RAF Marham I found myself administering over 500 personnel and I don't think anything can prepare you for that, but it suited my personality and skill sets.'

During this posting, Kristal was detached for four months to the Falkland Islands, an experience which left a lasting impression:

'I absolutely loved my time out in the Falklands and it was good experience doing my job but with Officers instead of aircrew. There was a great team atmosphere and I was out pretty much every night having fun. What more could a 19-year-old girl want?'

Her second posting, to RAF Aldergrove in Northern Ireland, wasn't the highlight of Kristal's career, as it didn't involve the personal interaction that she has enjoyed in her previous role. However, as ever, her pragmatic approach saw her through and she explains:

'One of the great aspects about a career in the RAF is the knowledge that in 2–3 years you will be doing a different job in a different area. Plus when I wasn't enjoying my post at RAF

Aldergrove I filled my time with adventure activities such as rock climbing and body surfing, which was cool.'

From Northern Ireland, Kristal was posted to RAF Honington, home to the RAF Regiment. There she was given the extra responsibility of mentoring a less experienced Personnel Administrator and says:

'It was good being able to pass on some of what I had already learned in the Pers Admin role. It gave me a sense of responsibility and allowed me to show my worth to my bosses.'

After a year at Honington, Kristal was posted to RAF Gibraltar, where she held the enviable role of PA to the Station Commander. A highly responsible job, Kristal was tasked with managing her boss's diary and acting as his mouthpiece in day-to-day communication. It was at RAF Gibraltar that Kristal was promoted to the rank of Corporal, an event which rates high on her list of achievements:

'Being promoted to Corporal has to rate as the highlight of my career so far. I felt so proud to be awarded the rank and it was proof that all my hard work and effort had paid off. I was also a small part in history being made when in 2005 I was part of the first ever female guard for the Convent of Gibraltar, the residence of the Governor, which is Gibraltar's equivalent of Buckingham Palace.'

And Kristal has certainly risen to every challenge, including a recent detachment to Afghanistan, where she was the sole Casualty and Compassionate Junior Non-Commissioned Officer for 7,000 British troops. The role involved communicating sometimes distressing and urgent news to personnel about family members and arranging for transportation back to the UK often at very short notice. Describing her time at Kandahar Air Base she says:

'My role in Afghanistan was, without a doubt, the hardest thing I have done in my life yet. Delivering bad news is emotionally draining and because of the time difference between there and the UK I was often required to jump into action at three or four in the morning. But it was also very rewarding because, when I managed to get someone home, perhaps in time to see their mother or father before they pass away, I knew I had done a good thing. It's not something I imagined I would be doing in my job as a Personnel Administrator but is certainly an experience I wouldn't trade now.'

Since returning from Afghanistan Kristal has been back in post at RAF Gibraltar but is now preparing for her next role as an NVQ Assessor. This post, based at the RAF School of Personnel Administration at Southwick Park in Portsmouth, will be a departure from anything Kristal has done so far, but by putting her 10 years of experience to good use Kristal will be ensuring that new recruits are doing what is required to gain the NVQs awarded to Personnel Administrators.

Reflecting on her time in the RAF Kristal says:

'It feels like only yesterday that I joined up, and experiences such as an expedition to the US, where I white-water-rafted in Pennsylvania and saw the sights of New York, to getting my powerboat licence whilst in Gibraltar, or being dangled out of a Sea King helicopter to flying in the passenger seat of a Wessex helicopter, have all added up to make my time in the RAF even more amazing than I thought it would be. My boss once said, if they cut me in half they would find a roundel and I have to agree they probably would because I love being part of the RAF.'

Joining age: 16–29

Pay after one year: £16,675

Open to: men or women

Usual service: 9 years

CHAPTER 9
TOOLS OF THE TRADE

One of the beauties of joining the Armed Forces is that you are provided with almost everything you'll need to do your job. From the uniform and kit to the technical skills you need to use it – it's all there. However, that doesn't mean that anyone can become a successful serviceman or -woman. To make use of all the equipment and training, you need to have the right potential – the basic skills and characteristics that your superiors will be able to work with. That doesn't mean that there's a single 'type' that you have to conform to – some people who seem born for the Armed Forces really aren't suitable at all.

Who you are or what your background is really doesn't matter. But you will need to show that you have a few personal characteristics and meet some simple eligibility requirements, which are outlined below.

WHAT YOU NEED

The work that the Armed Forces do is both physically and psychologically demanding. Whether you join the Army, Navy or RAF, your training will push you to the limit so that you are strong and alert enough to take responsibility for the lives of your colleagues and civilians in the field. For these reasons, you must be **physically and mentally fit** to join the Armed Forces, both now and for the foreseeable future. This doesn't mean that you have to be an Olympic athlete, just that you have the **basic ability to undergo the training** that will build you up to your peak.

For similar reasons, you must be of **the right age** to join up. This isn't ageism for the sake of it. Hundreds of years of experience have shown that if you're too young you probably won't have sufficient maturity to handle the challenge, while if you're too old you're less likely to respond to the training – even if you're still very fit – and less able to make a long-term commitment. **Precise age restrictions vary** between the three services and point of entry (officer, soldier, rating, trade), but generally speaking the minimum age is 16–17 years old and the maximum is around 33–36 years old. There are variations depending on specific job role requirements, so always check.

If you are to serve a country you will need to have an inherent 'loyalty' to that country, or at least a deeply ingrained affinity with it. This is primarily for security reasons. The precise details of nationality requirements can be complicated, but, put simply, to join the British Armed Forces **you need to be a citizen of the UK, a Commonwealth country or the Irish Republic.** It's also worth bearing in mind that some career paths are available only

DID YOU KNOW?

A career in the Armed Forces is like very few others in that lives sometimes actually do depend on the decisions you make.

to British citizens. A career in the Armed Forces is like very few others in that lives sometimes actually do depend on the decisions you make. Individually, this could mean the friend standing next to you on the battlefield, or the pilot flying the plane you've been maintaining. On a bigger scale, it could mean the people of the village you're delivering aid to, or the civilians living just a mile from where you're aiming your missiles. In such situations, being of **good character** is essential. Your colleagues and superiors must be able to **trust** you to do your job and carry out orders, while you must be able to treat the people you come into contact with, with respect and dignity, even if they are classified as the enemy.

Army, Navy and RAF training programmes are among the best in the world. They will teach you everything you need to know and provide you with many skills that will cross over into civilian life. However, if you don't have the **basic ability and willingness to learn**, they will probably be lost on you. **You don't need a lot of qualifications** for all ranks, just the kind of literacy, numeracy and logical reasoning skills necessary to understand what you are being taught, and the awareness to take it on board. Check each job role for entry requirements.

Being in the Armed Forces isn't easy. Whether you're going through the selection process or basic training, or if you're on exercise or operational deployment, it's never less than a challenge. Not only do you need to have the ability to learn, you also need **self-discipline**, as well as **commitment, enthusiasm** and **motivation** – they will keep you going through the long hours, the physical strain, the mental pressure and the crises in confidence. Your team-mates will be depending on you. If you're not a **team player**, you can forget about a career in the Armed Forces. Almost without exception, if you join up you will never work alone. You will always be dependent on someone else, and someone else will always be depending on you.

People **working together** – that's how the Army, Navy and RAF are able to be much more than the sums of their parts. While the above are the key attributes, you'll need to enjoy a successful career in the Armed Forces, if you have ambitions to become an Officer there are some additional skills and qualities that you should bear in mind. Together these make up the key quality of **leadership**.

LEADERSHIP – THE KEY TO BEING AN OFFICER

Taking command of a group of highly trained men and women is a daunting prospect, especially if a number of them are older and more experienced than you are. If you don't show the required confidence and charisma, then you'll be at risk of losing their respect, which will affect morale and the overall effectiveness of the unit. It's difficult to say exactly what confidence and charisma are, but if you're satisfied that you have them then you probably do.

We mentioned earlier that in the Armed Forces the decisions you make could have grave consequences. The pressure of such decision making tends to be more intense for officers because they are in a position where they have to make more decisions, more often. Two qualities come into play here: **good judgement**, which helps you to make the right decision under stress; and **decisiveness**, which gives you the courage of your convictions and allows you to move with purpose, rather than with damaging uncertainty.

DID YOU KNOW?

It wasn't until 1838 that British soldiers were given separate boots for their right and left feet. Until then, they had boots that could be worn on either foot.

Being a good leader is also about taking **responsibility**. You will not only have to trust yourself to make the right decision but also be prepared to accept the blame if things go wrong. It works both ways and taking responsibility also means getting the credit for things going well.

Finally, you cannot be an effective Officer without having good **communication skills**, and these are vital throughout the chain of command. It is particularly important that those in charge are able to get their thoughts and orders across clearly and effectively. This not only ensures that people know exactly what they have to do; it can also serve to **motivate** and **inspire**, two qualities that can be the difference between the success and failure of an exercise or operation. Having looked at the qualities the Armed Forces do want their members to have, we'll take a look at those things they certainly don't want!

The importance of communication skills is demonstrated in the very early stages of selection. For every Force, and for whichever

level you are being selected, you will have to pass **an interview.**
There may be more than one person interviewing you. For the
Royal Navy/Royal Marines Officer entry, this will be with the
Admiralty Board, and to be an officer in the Army, it will be
the Army Officer Selection Board. To prepare, find out as much as
you can about interview skills, what the interview will consist of,
and be prepared to talk about why you want to be selected.

WHAT MIGHT COUNT AGAINST YOU

Having established an overall picture of a person who is well
suited to the Armed Forces, it is also important to run through
some of the factors that may prevent you from joining up or from
building a successful career once you're there. You should bear the
following in mind before making the decision to apply.

▶ For the Army and Royal Navy, **you will need to pass a full
medical inspection**, and the Royal Marines includes physical
tests within its Potential Officers Course. For the RAF you will
need to pass a medical and fitness test. **Learn to swim:**
obviously important for the Royal Navy and Royal Marines, but
you never know when you might need this survival skill. For the
Royal Marines it is also important that you are **able to work at
heights and able to carry weights**. You may have to cope
with cramped living conditions on board ships and submarines,
which can be an issue if you are **claustrophobic**.

▶ Being fit for duty doesn't just mean being able to run long
distances or carry heavy loads; it also covers **certain medical
conditions** that may preclude you from joining one of the
Armed Forces. For example, epilepsy, diabetes, certain gastric
disorders, rheumatoid arthritis, severe headaches, chronic eye
problems and asthma are all reasons the RAF gives for rejecting
applications. **Eyesight standards and colour blindness** can
affect entry to certain roles in all the Armed Forces. You must

check your chosen service's specific restrictions carefully or risk disappointment later.

▶ You may also find that for certain jobs you will have to meet a **minimum height requirement**. For example, to be a rating with the Royal Navy you must be no shorter than 151.5 cm, and your weight must be in proportion to your height. Again, you should check with each service before applying if you are concerned.

▶ In addition to the rules on nationality, to be eligible to join the Armed Forces you should normally have been living in the UK for a number of years (usually 3–5 years) before making an application. Even if you are a British citizen, **if you live overseas** it may be difficult, though still possible, to join up.

▶ A little independence is a good quality to possess, even in a team environment. It helps you to be self-reliant and to take responsibility for your actions. However, the services are no place for loners. Whether it's through **arrogance**, **shyness** or just a **general dislike of other people**, if you'd rather be alone, the Armed Forces are not for you. You must be prepared to be sociable and cooperative, not aloof or difficult. A sense of humour helps, too!

▶ Similarly, you cannot afford to be **excessively timid**. It's OK to be unsure of yourself, especially when you're just starting out, and not everyone is built to be the life and soul of the party, but if you lack the courage to work through your fears, your performance – and more importantly, that of your team – will suffer. You don't have to be particularly bold or loud, just able to hold your own and prepared to do your best.

▶ Finally, you should be aware that spent and unspent **criminal convictions** (including time spent in prison, a young offenders institution or on probation) **for certain types of offences** may mean that you are ineligible for some parts of the Armed Forces. Seek advice from an Armed Forces Careers Office if you think this may apply to you.

QUIZ

If you've read through the last few pages, you should have quite
a good idea of whether you're cut out for a career in the Armed
Forces or not. If you think you are, why not test your knowledge
and suitability a little further by completing the following short
quiz. For each question, just choose which option you think is
correct or the closest to what you think your response would be,
and compare it with the answers at the end of the chapter. Don't
worry if you get any questions wrong; it's only meant to be a bit of
fun. The serious stuff will start when you apply to join up for real.

1 **To join the Army Cadet Force you need to be aged
between:**

   A. 16 and 18.

   B. 14 and 16.

   C. 12 and 18.

2 **A member of your unit has just recorded the slowest time
of the day on the assault course and must do it again.
How do you respond? Do you:**

   A. Return to the barracks, shower and prepare yourself for an
evening in the mess?

   B. Remain outside and shout encouragement to your team-mate
from the sidelines?

   C. Support your team-mate by running the assault course with them?

3 **After a long day's training, your kit fails inspection and
you are reprimanded in front of all your mates. Do you:**

   A. Withstand the humiliation, take the criticism on board and
resolve to do better next time?

   B. Take it as a sign that you're not good enough and leave the
services at the earliest possible opportunity?

C. Argue with your superior officer that it's not fair because you were tired?

---

4 **Which of the following is not a letter in the phonetic alphabet used by the British Armed Forces?**
A. Romeo?
B. Juliet?
C. Othello?

---

5 **Why would you never say 'repeat' into a military radio?**
A. Because it may lead to wasted ammunition and possible casualties?
B. Because your superiors won't tolerate having to say the same thing twice?
C. Because the military word for 'say again' is 'encore'?

---

6 **The UK is procuring two new Aircraft Carriers for the Royal Navy, HMS *Prince of Wales* and:**
A. HMS *Camilla*?
B. HMS *Prince William*?
C. HMS *Queen Elizabeth*?

---

7 **The Royal Marines Corps' motto '*per mare per terram*' means what?**
A. 'We're going to get you'?
B. 'By sea, by land'?
C. 'The best, the most terrifying'?

---

8 **You are enjoying some well-deserved rest and recuperation in a civilian bar a few miles from base. Another customer starts trouble with you and your colleagues for being 'warmongers'. Do you:**
A. Calmly explain the true nature of your job and the services the Armed Forces provide around the world?
B. Forcefully tell them that, without you, they wouldn't be safe in their bed at night?
C. Punch them?

9 **The Apache helicopter was first used in combat during which conflict?**

A. The Falklands crisis?

B. The invasion of Panama?

C. The Gulf War?

10 **What does NATO stand for?**

A. North Atlantic Treaty Organisation.

B. National Armed Technology Organisation.

C. National Alliance against Terror Organisation.

ANSWERS

1. C. Check with your nearest Army Careers Office for contact details.

2. C (or, if not possible, B). Good morale and team spirit is the life-blood of the Armed Forces, and you should never leave a team-mate to feel isolated and alone.

3. A. It is crucial that you show resilience and discipline, even in the face of stinging criticism. If things go wrong in the field, you'll just have to get on with it and won't be able to give up or argue that it's not fair. Besides, your mates won't think any the less of you – they'll all go through the same experience at some stage.

4. C. The phonetic alphabet uses words to represent each letter, making it more difficult to confuse words when they are spelt out over the radio. The American phonetic alphabet is, perhaps surprisingly, very different from the one used in the UK.

5. A. By saying 'repeat' you are issuing the order to carry out the last action again, which could mean firing at a target where there are now people.

6. C. It is estimated that the two aircraft carriers will cost £3.9 billion and they are due to enter service sometime between 2015 and 2018.

7. B. The Royal Marines are the Navy's commandos, highly trained experts in amphibious, jungle, mountain and arctic warfare. They are deployed from the sea directly into the action on the ground, hence the motto

8. A. The best thing you can do both for yourself and the image of the Armed Forces is not rise to the bait. If you resort to violence, you'll only be proving their point.

9. B. Apache helicopters were first used in combat during the 1989 invasion of Panama, 'Operation Just Cause'. They were later used in the Gulf War and carried out the first attack of 'Desert Storm' in Iraq in 1991.

10. A. The North Atlantic Treaty Organisation was formed shortly after the end of the Second World War to counter the threat of Soviet invasion of Western Europe. Membership of NATO comprises 10 countries from Western Europe, plus Canada and America. Its mandate is to provide a common defence for the European and Atlantic areas, and to address common issues faced by the member countries.

CHAPTER 10
FAQs

By now, you should be aware of what it takes to become part of the Armed Forces and how, through a wide range of different career opportunities, your work will contribute to the safety and quality of life of people all over the world. But what about your life? Apart from the satisfaction that comes through knowing that you're helping people and serving your country, what's in it for you? What can you expect day to day? How will it affect your lifestyle and your long-term plans?

The rest of this chapter answers some of the most frequently asked questions about the personal aspects of working for the Armed Forces. It should help you to make up your mind whether it really is a career for you.

Q **Once I've joined up, can I move up the promotion ladder quickly?**

A One of the main attractions of working in the Armed Forces is the availability of structured career progression.

The way the Army, Navy and RAF are organised means that talent and hard work are always rewarded. The speed and direction in which you can potentially progress vary considerably according to such factors as the rank at which you join, your chosen specialisation, your education and qualifications, your leadership ability, your performance, your experience and so on. Theoretically, anything is possible – if you're good enough you could race through the ranks – but it depends on what's available. And throughout your career, you will be required to undertake certain training and gain qualifications before you can progress. You will of course receive all the help you need to do this.

Is it a 9 to 5 job?

It varies.

The work of the Armed Forces is determined by the responsibilities they must fulfil, and these don't necessarily fit in with your family or social commitments!

In the RAF, personnel typically work Monday to Friday, 9am to 5pm – but may be on call at all times. Hours could be longer if you are involved in operations and detachments (being away from home for several months). As a rating in the Royal Navy, you could be on call 24 hours a day and work a shift system which includes weekends and public holidays. Generally speaking, you should be able to 'clock off' and 'go home' at the end of most days, even if you're living in barracks. You'll probably never switch off completely, but every effort is made to make it as normal a life for you as possible.

Will I get time off for holidays?

Of course.

While joining the Armed Forces is a big commitment on your part, it's not like signing your life away. Indeed, regular breaks are seen as an important part of maintaining a fit and motivated fighting force. As such, you can expect to get around 30 days' paid leave a year, which compares well to other jobs. However, your choice of when to take time off must be planned well in advance and will be limited by the requirements of your job. For instance, if you're needed to defend an overseas territory from invasion, you're needed – simple as that. Enemy forces won't call off an attack just because you want to go to Ibiza! And you are likely to miss the odd Christmas or two with your family, although this is not always seen as a bad thing!

How much can I expect to earn?

As with all these questions it really depends on which service you join, what your specialisation is, your experience, performance and rank.

However, pay is structured according to set scales, so you can be secure in the knowledge that you will be getting a fair deal. To give you a rough idea, new recruits to the Army joining as soldiers receive around £13,000 per annum (year), while Lance Corporals can earn up to £27,600. In the Navy, new ratings also get about £13,000, depending on their particular job, and Lieutenants can earn from £36,000 to £43,000 (there are also additional incentive payments for specific duties). The RAF pays a new airman/air-woman a minimum of £13,000, rising to over £16,000. Pilot Officers start at £23,475 and Flying Officers can earn between £28,000 and £31,188 per annum.

In all three services, each rank has its own pay scale that you can move up over time and with promotion, with senior officers receiving upwards of £50,000–70,000 in the later years of their careers. Generally speaking, though, pay scales are set to reflect civilian wages for similar jobs, with a little extra on top to compensate for the special circumstances and importance of the Armed Forces. And as an added bonus, you will often get your living expenses (accommodation and food) subsidised or paid for you.

How long will I have to join up for?

The important thing to remember when you join up is that you're not signing your life away.

If at some stage you find that the Army, Navy or RAF is not for you, it is possible to leave. However, it's not as simple as just jacking it in. You do need to make a minimum commitment to make it worthwhile for the Ministry of Defence to invest thousands of pounds of taxpayers' money in your training, equipment, accommodation, food and salary. Again, the time you commit depends on the service and the level at which you join. For example, if you join the RAF, you'll be asked to join for a minimum length of service depending on your job. Usually it's between 6 and 12 years. Airmen/airwomen have the right to leave without penalty three years after completing basic training. If you are under 18 and 3 months, you can leave provided you register your need to leave with your superiors before your 18th birthday. In the Army, for an

Active Duty Soldier, length of service can range from 2 to 6 years. In the Royal Navy the length of service will depend on the role and which part of the Navy or Royal Marines you are serving in, but if you request to leave you will need to work a notice period of 12 months. You are normally required to serve for around 2.5 years after training. Check with each Armed service so that you are aware of your rights in this matter. Remember that if you receive sponsorship and you leave early, you may be asked to pay some or all of it back!

Will I be able to work abroad?

Almost certainly.

The very nature of the Armed Forces and their responsibilities means that right now there are thousands of servicemen and -women working overseas, either on short-term operational detachments or permanent postings in barracks such as those in Germany and Cyprus. You may not have much choice in where you travel to, and it may mean spending long periods of time away from your family and friends, but there aren't many better ways of getting paid to see the world.

What can I expect to get out of the Armed Forces personally?

Given the size and scope of the Armed Forces and the kind of work they do, pretty much anything!

Unique experiences; a sense of achievement; doing good; serving your country and contributing to world peace; developing courage and endurance; friendships that last a lifetime; a ready-made social life; new skills and qualifications ... the list goes on. You can see the world, live in another country, meet interesting people, experience other cultures, encounter new ways of thinking, improve your fitness ... The potential is there for you to have it all – professionally and personally.

DID YOU KNOW?

The Beatles' music publisher, Dick James, was a former Army Corps musician.

How will the public see me?

The political aspects of the Armed Forces, and in particular warfare, have varying degrees of popularity.

Most people you meet will respect the work that servicemen and women do and the sacrifices being made on their behalf. Of course, there'll always be the odd person who'll take a stereotypical view of Armed Forces personnel, but these are in the minority, and your real friends will still see you as an individual and be there for you.

What kinds of dangers will I face?

Obviously, there are potentially serious risks to your safety in joining the Armed Forces. You will be given professional training.

The training that you'll be given and the equipment you'll have at your disposal are designed to minimise any risks to your health and safety. So whether you're flying a plane, maintaining a ship's engine or engaging the enemy on the ground, you will be in the best possible position, given the circumstances, to use equipment effectively and make calm and rational decisions should danger arise.

What about the discipline?

Everyone in the Armed Forces needs to take orders.

Many also need to give them. A lot of people don't find this an easy concept to come to terms with, making the transition from a relaxed and 'ill-disciplined' civilian life to the tight ships run by the Army, Navy and Air Force a difficult one. However, order and discipline are there for a reason. They ensure safety and get things done. Once you get used to them and develop a full appreciation of why they are necessary, not only will you not mind them so much, you will also most likely come to welcome and even rely on them.

Will I cope with feeling homesick?

This is quite a common experience and usually fades once you get used to a new routine and make new friends who are going through similar feelings. However, it can be difficult initially. If you continue to find it hard, you must talk to someone during training, and let your family know, so that you can receive support and not become depressed. Other new recruits will be missing their families too and you will support each other. It is perfectly natural to miss people you are close to, and this happens again and again when leave comes to an end or you are called to serve abroad. New technology does make it easier to keep in touch, but you need to remember that being absent some of the time is part of the lifestyle you are choosing.

CHAPTER 11
TRAINING

Throughout this book we have mentioned examples of the huge variety of different jobs available in the Armed Forces – jobs that cater for all interests and abilities. At this stage, it's probably difficult for you to know exactly what you want to do with a career in the Army, Navy or Air Force, but it's never too early to start thinking about your options.

On joining, you may find that you're particularly well suited to one of the junior ranks and want to continue in that capacity, or may grow to like the idea of operating on the front line.

Perhaps you'll choose to pursue an interest in a particular specialist area – be it engineering, healthcare, IT, music or whatever – or a particular course of training. You may find you have a talent for teaching other servicemen and -women or that you're particularly well cut out for the management and leadership challenges of the senior ranks. You may be particularly keen to experience life in a foreign country and apply for a detachment or posting overseas, or you might prefer the comfort of a job in an office... In short, the choices are nearly endless.

Your time in the Armed Forces will provide you with a range of highly sought-after transferable skills, not to mention specialist expertise and experience that will set you up for a long and rewarding career.

No matter what vocational training you have completed in the past or how many GCSEs, A levels, diplomas or degrees you have got, there is a route in. Even if you have nothing in the way of formal attainment to your name, there are still roles to which you could be ideally suited. But, of course, the more qualifications you have, the better your potential to learn and the more entry points and roles you'll have to choose from. So if you have a particular interest or ambition that you'd like to pursue in the Armed Forces, it may help to get some qualifications first.

DID YOU KNOW?

The Armed Forces give you access to just about as many different potential career paths as civilian life.

Below, we'll be looking at the various entry routes into the services, according to your particular situation or set of circumstances. You should note that opportunities and requirements change frequently, so you must also contact the Armed Forces directly and check out their websites (given in Further information).

QUALIFICATIONS

Due to the complexity regarding entry requirements for the plethora of jobs within the Armed Forces, this chapter will deal with just the main points of entry, relevant qualifications, training and progression opportunities. It will also refer to forms of financial assistance available from the Armed Forces, but you must check these out too, nearer the time you may be thinking of joining.

The more qualifications you have, the better your potential to learn and the more entry points and roles you'll have to choose from.

THE ARMY

Army soldier

Army entrance test

Taken by all applicants, this is a touch-screen, common sense, multiple choice test that takes approximately 30 minutes to complete. It tests whether you are suitable for Army training and the kinds of roles suitable.

Selection Centre

Following the test, you will spend 2–3 days at the Army Development and Selection Centre. This includes a medical and physical assessment, and you can find out more about what is involved.

Junior entrants 16 years to 17 years and 1 month

1. You can attend the 42-week course at the Army Foundation College in Harrogate. This includes 23 weeks' military training, 5 weeks' leadership and 14 weeks' vocational training, leading to NVQ Levels 2–3. Intakes are twice a year, in September and January.
2. You can join the Army Training Regiment at Bassingbourn, which includes 20 weeks' military training, a lot of sport and industry-recognised qualifications. Phase 2 training is in specific regiments.

Basic training

Basic training involves drill skills, map reading, first aid, weapons handling, field craft, night training, camouflage techniques, target practice, fitness tests and adventure training.

When you have completed Phase 1 you have a 'Passing Out' parade and move on to your regiment or corps to begin Phase 2 specialist training, which varies in length according to your job role, and involves studying relevant qualifications up to Level 3.

Progression

You can gain promotion and train as an officer, if you show leadership potential. You can apply to the AOSB for the full commissioning course, or you could move up through the non-commissioned officer ranks and be selected for 'Late Entry' commission after nine years. Women can't apply for a commission in the Household Cavalry, the Royal Armoured Corps or the Infantry.

Welbeck, the Army's residential sixth form college, is the ideal platform from which to become an Officer in one of the technical corps.

The University Officer Training Corps provides you with access to military, adventurous and leadership training while you are still at university.

There are **Army education centres** spread across the UK and Cyprus, including training regiments and colleges and over 100 Army Learning Centres, which are mobile units that use the latest developments in online and distance learning to help you study.

The Army also runs schemes to provide soldiers with financial support for further learning. With the new **Further Education Bursary Scheme (FEBS)**, you maybe eligible to earn a cash award whilst studying. The commitment you make in return is to spend a minimum of four years in the Army. Check the Army website for a list of participating colleges or call 08457 300 111 to speak to an Army Careers Adviser.

Army officer

Entry Band 4. For direct entry to a commission, you will need a minimum of two A levels and seven GCSEs (A*–C). In Scotland, this is three H grades and seven S grades (1–3), including English, maths, and either a science or foreign language subject. Applicants offering alternative equivalent qualifications (e.g. applied A levels, BTEC National awards, the new Higher Diplomas) will be considered on their own merits.

Entry Band 5. For a degree course leading to a commission, you will need at least 2 A levels and 5 GCSEs (A*–C). In Scotland, this is 3 H grades and 2 other S grades (1–3), including English and maths. Again, relevant alternatives will be considered on their own merits, and, in any case, for university entrance, the exact requirements will depend on the degree being taken, so you must check this out.

Type of degree. Any degree discipline is acceptable, although professional qualifications (e.g. medicine, dentistry, veterinary science, law or engineering) will be required for certain specialisms.

Obtaining a commission
Army Officer Selection Board
Applicants attend the Board to undergo a series of written exams and physical tests (including a medical), designed to measure leadership potential. Check age and nationality requirements before applying. For example, if you join under the age of 18 years, you could leave on your 22nd birthday. If you join over the age of 18, your commission lasts 4 years 3 months, but in both cases you could choose to stay in for a maximum of 22 years.

The Royal Military Academy, Sandhurst (RMAS)
The Commissioning Course (CC) at Sandhurst is for 11 months. Here you will be trained to enhance skills such as decision making, negotiating, self-confidence, mental agility, leadership and communication. You will receive specialist training in the corps in which you are to serve. After passing the CC, you will receive your commission and leave RMAS to join your corps or regiment as a Second Lieutenant. You would then begin specialist junior officer training to prepare you to lead a troop or platoon. You would receive ongoing training to help you develop your skills to gain further promotion.

Professionally Qualified Officer (PQO) route
If you are already professionally trained (doctor, barrister, dentist, nurse, etc.), and possess the required qualifications for

these professions, you can apply to be considered for the fast-track Professionally Qualified Officer's course which takes four weeks.

THE ROYAL NAVY/ ROYAL MARINES

Navy rating

The Navy recruits around 4,000 ratings per year. All applicants must pass **selection tests** in literacy, numeracy, reasoning and comprehension. There are specific qualifications for certain trades. As so many trades are available you will need to contact the Royal Navy Careers Office to check which qualifications you will need and the types of vocational training you can pursue. In addition, applicants should also be of a minimum height of 151.5 cm, with weight in proportion to height. Learn to swim if you can't already do so.

Entry bands

Band 1. For many jobs, no qualifications are required. GCSEs or equivalent, at any level, would be useful, though. An interest in science and technology is useful.

Band 2. For some trades, 1–3 GCSEs/S grades, including English, maths, geography, physics or a suitable science (or equivalent), are needed.

Band 3. 4–5 GCSEs (A*–C), S grades (1–3), including subjects such as English, maths, geography, physics or a suitable science subject or equivalent, depending on the trade chosen.

Officer/Royal Marine entry bands

Entry for full/short service commission
Band 4. 2 A levels and 3 GCSEs (A*–C) or 3 H grades and 3 S grades (1–3) including maths and English.

Band 5. For degree courses leading to graduate entry, 2–3 A levels and some GCSEs (A*–C), or 3–4 H grades and some S grades (1–3), including English and maths.

Basic training

This is at HMS *Raleigh* at Torpoint (Plymouth). You will progress to specific training for your chosen trade, often at a different naval establishment. You will then be posted to a ship or shore base.

Further training/study

Training is mostly on the job but you can also study for national educational qualifications including NVQs, degrees and professional awards. Promotion prospects improve with further training and for special skills and service (e.g. in submarines). Around 25% of ratings become Officers. Most ratings join for 18 years or up to the age of 40, whichever is the later, but you can leave 2.5 years after completion of your initial training.

Royal Navy officer

About 500 new officers are recruited per year.

Basic entry

You will need 5 GCSEs (A*–C) or S grades (1–3), including English and maths, plus 2 A levels or 3 H grades.

Direct graduate entry

You can apply for this if you have a degree. However, for the specialist occupations such as doctor, air engineering officer, etc., then relevant degrees are sought. Check with Armed Forces Careers personnel.

The Admiralty Board Interview

This involves a 2-day assessment, which includes interviews and tests in communication, maths, mental agility, spatial orientation and physical fitness.

Basic training

This would be at the Britannia Royal Naval College at Dartmouth, and would take about 12 months (depending on your specialism). It would include experience on a warship, management, leadership and teamwork training. This would be followed by further training in your specialism. See the Royal Navy website for details. New opportunities arise every 2–3 years to move ship or change shore base.

Your initial commission would be for 12 years. You could leave during initial training, once you have given 14 days' notice. After this, you can leave after 3–5 years' service, depending on your specialism.

Progression

If you pass your training period and perform well, you would be promoted to Lieutenant. The next progression would be to Lieutenant Commander and possibly beyond!

The Royal Marines

Entry is extremely competitive and selection is based on aptitude, character and personality. Entry is only open to males between 17 and 26 years old (the upper age limit varies).

Selection

Applicants attend a Potential Officers Course (POC) and, if suitable, are invited to attend an Admiralty Interview Board (AIB). These stages both include physical and academic tests designed to assess leadership potential.

Training

Phase 1. The first 54 weeks are spent at the Commando Training Centre at Lympstone in Devon, covering initial, military, amphibious and commando training, lasting 32 weeks and leading to the award of the Marines' Green Beret. The rest of the training develops officer and leadership skills.

Phase 2. This lasts a year and involves command of a troop of 28 commandos in an operational unit.

Opportunities

Marines officers tend to start with a short-term commission of 8 years, but may be able to serve until they are 55 years old. They must serve at least 3 years after completing Phase 2. The promotion structure is clearly defined, and pay increases accordingly. Beyond certain ranks it is based on selection.

THE ROYAL AIR FORCE

Non-Commissioned Aircrew (Weapon Systems Operator)

Selection

The selection tests include comprehension, practical initiative, fitness and a medical.

Basic training

Basic training is 9 weeks at RAF Halton in Buckinghamshire, covering military skills and improving physical fitness. You then move to RAF Cranwell for a leadership course lasting 10 weeks. This covers communication, administration and organisational skills. Next, you begin specialist training, which will vary according to your chosen role. After this you are posted to an Operational Conversion Unit to receive on-the-job training for your aircraft duties.

Progression

You will be promoted to Acting Sergeant when you start aircrew flying training, followed by promotion to full Sergeant as you take on your full duties. Later, you could move on to become Flight Sergeant and Master Aircrew. You can apply to become a commissioned officer.

RAF Airman/Airwoman

Entry and selection

You will need to pass a series of aptitude tests, including practical initiative. For some of the trades you will need GCSEs and BTEC or City & Guilds qualifications. Women are not able to join the RAF Regiment, which includes combat.

Basic and further training

This begins with a 9-week course at RAF Halton in Buckinghamshire, covering weapons handling, survival techniques, physical fitness and general service knowledge. Training in your specific trade takes place between 3 weeks and 18 months, depending on the skills needed, and you would work towards NVQs, BTEC or City & Guilds awards. The average signing up commitment is between 6 and 12 years.

Progression

After specialist training, you will be promoted to Leading Airman/Airwoman and then to senior, usually after 1 year's service. After this, promotion is on merit. You can apply at any time to become a commissioned officer.

RAF officer

The RAF recruits new officers every year, but competition is strong. Many applicants are graduates.

Basic entry

You must have at least 5 GCSEs (A*–C), or S grades (1–3), plus 2 A levels, or 3 H grades, including English and maths, or equivalent, to be discussed when applying.

Selection

In addition to the usual nationality, medical and fitness requirements, you must pass a series of selection tests, including interviews, at the RAF College, Cranwell, in Lincolnshire.

Officer training

Selection is followed by a 30-week Initial Officer Training course at Cranwell. If you join professionally qualified (e.g. as a doctor or dentist), your training may be reduced to 12 weeks. This further training includes fitness, lectures and practical exercises in leadership and management, defence studies and RAF service knowledge. You would then go on to specialist training in your chosen branch.

Progression
You will often be able to study for civilian qualifications, enabling you to progress with careers outside of the Armed Forces. Promotion is based on length of service to begin with, and is from Pilot Officer to Flying Officer and then Flight Lieutenant. Graduates often progress more quickly through the ranks. Promotion beyond Flight Lieutenant is by competitive selection.

FUNDING

Army

Army Scholarship Scheme: These can be received whilst studying A levels/H grades at school, with the requirement to serve in the Army for at least 3 years after leaving school. **The University Officer Training Corps** offers experience and pay, but does not require a commitment to future service.

Cadetships: These are awarded to those studying to be doctors, nurses and vets. You basically receive a salary whilst studying, but must serve in the army for a minimum of 5 years after graduation.

Army Undergraduate Bursary Scheme: University students who receive a bursary must serve in the Army for 3 years after completing the degree course.

Royal Air Force

RAF sixth form scholarships, university bursaries, medical, dental or engineering scholarships are available. Check the RAF website or ring the Advice line for more details.

Royal Navy

The Royal Navy offers undergraduate scholarships and bursaries such as the Defence Technical Undergraduate Scheme (value up to £5,500), a Golden Hello for undergraduate engineers (value £12,000), Medical and Dental Cadetships, and Standard and Technical Bursaries for undergraduate students (value £1,500 or £4,000), and the Undergraduate Cadetship Entry bursary (value £15,954). Any career in the submarine service may attract a Golden Hello of up to £5,000. Specialist pay is also available to aircrew, hydrographers and mine clearance divers.

As funding arrangements change very regularly, always check with the Armed Forces Careers Offices for updates on schemes and levels of funding available.

NEW VOCATIONAL DIPLOMAS

From September 2009, 14- to 19-year-olds can choose to study from up to 10 Diploma subjects over 2 years, in subjects such as Engineering, IT, Health and Development, Creative and Media, Construction and the Built Environment. Find out which ones are coming up in your school or college. Diplomas are offered at different academic levels, and it would be worth checking with your Armed Forces adviser about which ones will be acceptable for different occupations.

FIGURE 11
ACCESS TO ... THE ARMED FORCES

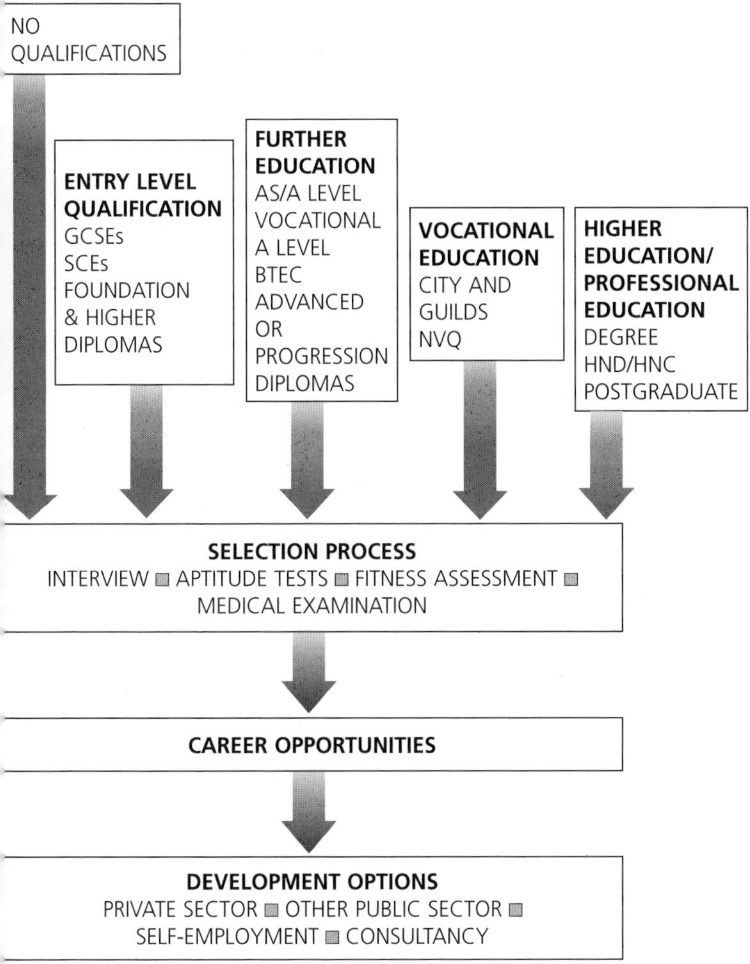

NO
QUALIFICATIONS

**ENTRY LEVEL
QUALIFICATION**
GCSEs
SCEs
FOUNDATION
& HIGHER
DIPLOMAS

**FURTHER
EDUCATION**
AS/A LEVEL
VOCATIONAL
A LEVEL
BTEC
ADVANCED
OR
PROGRESSION
DIPLOMAS

**VOCATIONAL
EDUCATION**
CITY AND
GUILDS
NVQ

**HIGHER
EDUCATION/
PROFESSIONAL
EDUCATION**
DEGREE
HND/HNC
POSTGRADUATE

SELECTION PROCESS
INTERVIEW ▣ APTITUDE TESTS ▣ FITNESS ASSESSMENT ▣
MEDICAL EXAMINATION

CAREER OPPORTUNITIES

DEVELOPMENT OPTIONS
PRIVATE SECTOR ▣ OTHER PUBLIC SECTOR ▣
SELF-EMPLOYMENT ▣ CONSULTANCY

CAREER OPPORTUNITIES

As you'll have seen, the Armed Forces represent a career with many and varied opportunities for advancement. As you go through your training and build up some experience, you will gradually discover where your strengths and preferences lie and will be able to map out a career path. Figure 12 is a simple illustration of how your options and the rank structure will open up with training.

FIGURE 12
CAREER OPPORTUNITIES

JOIN UP/MINIMAL EXPERIENCE AND QUALIFICATIONS
SOLDIER ▪ RATING ▪ TRADE

MORE EXPERIENCE/SPECIALIST EXPERIENCE/EARN
QUALIFICATIONS
NON-COMMISSIONED OFFICER

FURTHER EXPERIENCE/TRAINING/
QUALIFICATIONS
COMMISSIONED OFFICER

CHAPTER 12
THE LAST WORD

If you've made it this far, then the chances are that you've decided whether a career in the Armed Forces is for you. If you think it is, then congratulations – a lot of people can't stomach the idea of following orders or getting up early or going on long runs, but if you can, then it's a sign that you may well have what it takes. And it'll be worth the effort, too.

To be part of the Armed Forces is to be part of a group of organisations that is working to make the world a better and safer place for everyone. Even with the range of training and career opportunities available, that is still the most rewarding aspect of the job. But before you start looking at your options in more detail by talking to an Armed Forces Careers Officer or visiting the various websites listed at the back of the book, here's a final, fun checklist to see if you have chosen wisely.

Tick Yes or No

Are you comfortable dealing with people in authority?	☐ Yes	☐ No
Do you like living and working closely with other people?	☐ Yes	☐ No
Are you able to get up early in the morning?	☐ Yes	☐ No
Are you happy to take responsibility for your actions?	☐ Yes	☐ No

Do you like physical activity?	☐ Yes ☐ No
Do you want a job that helps people?	☐ Yes ☐ No
Do you want to see the world?	☐ Yes ☐ No
Are you motivated to learn new skills?	☐ Yes ☐ No

If you answered 'yes' to all these questions, then CONGRATULATIONS! YOU'VE CHOSEN THE RIGHT CAREER! If you answered 'no' to any of these questions, then this may not actually be the career for you. You may prefer to think of some other, similar options. For example, what about joining the police service or the fire brigade?

CHAPTER 13
FURTHER INFORMATION

There is so much on offer in the way of career opportunities in the Armed Forces, it is essential that you take a much closer look than the space in this guide allows for. In this section, you will find a wealth of sources of information to help you with this task – websites, telephone numbers, addresses, and other books and publications ... Have a look at as many as you can before making your final decision: no matter how much you think you know, there's always something to surprise you in the Armed Forces.

USEFUL WEBSITES

The three main Armed Forces careers websites are excellent, containing page after page of detailed information as well as lots of colourful and informative features, including film clips, to help you decide where you might best fit in. They are:

- ▶ www.armyjobs.co.uk
- ▶ www.rnjobs.co.uk
- ▶ www.rafcareers.com

You will also be able to use these websites to make an enquiry about joining. For more general information about each of the services, you can visit their individual websites.

▶ www.army.mod.uk or http://www.armyonline.mod.uk for the Army online Careers Office, where you can have live chat sessions with serving soldiers.

▶ www.royal-navy.mod.uk

▶ www.raf.mod.uk

▶ www.royalmarines.mod.uk

If, on the other hand, you're interested in the reservist option, you should check out the respective reserve forces' websites.

▶ www.ta.mod.uk

▶ www.ms-sc.org

▶ www.rauxaf.mod.uk

And if you're too young to join up at the moment, you may want to check out what the Cadet Forces have to offer.

▶ www.armycadets.com

▶ www.sea-cadets.org

▶ www.aircadets.org

Ministry of Defence

And if you'd like to find out more about the current thinking behind the Armed Forces, and the range of civilian jobs on offer in the defence industry, your first port of call should be the Ministry of Defence website:

▶ www.mod.uk

Merchant Navy opportunities

Apply direct to shipping companies for details of recruitment and training and for the availability of sponsorship:

▶ www.careeersatsea.org/apply

or contact Careers at Sea, 12 Carthusian St, London EC1M 6EZ Tel: 0800 085 0973.

Marine-related and most other types of degree course are listed on the UCAS site:

▶ www.ucas.co.uk

ARMED FORCES CAREERS ADVISERS

While they're extremely useful, there's a limit to how much you can get out of websites, even ones as good as the Armed Forces. Sometimes you just need to talk to an expert. For this, you can get in touch with your nearest Armed Forces Careers Advisers, by phone, fax, post or in person – you'll find them all over the country and you're welcome to pop in without an appointment.

To find out where the nearest one is to your home, call:

▶ The Royal Navy   08456 075555
▶ The British Army   08457 300111
▶ The Royal Air Force   08456 05 5555

Most of the addresses are also posted on the Armed Forces individual websites.

Welbeck College

Welbeck College, the Defence Sixth Form College, has a programme specifically designed to prepare students for a career in the Armed Forces.

Forest Road
Woodhouse
Loughborough
Leicestershire
LE12 8WD
www.welbeck.mod.uk